Shawls, Stoles and Scarves

Alice Mackrell

The Costume Accessories Series
General Editor: Dr Aileen Ribeiro ✓

B.T. BATSFORD LTD
LONDON

In fond memory of Madeleine Nicolas,
friend and enthusiastic teacher and artistic
réalisateur of so many delightful exhibitions
at the Musée de La Mode et du Costume in
Paris

© Alice Mackrell 1986
First published 1986

ISBN 0 7134 4876 8

Typeset by Tek-Art Ltd, Kent
and printed in Great Britain by
Anchor Brendon Ltd
Tiptree, Essex
for the publishers
B.T. Batsford Ltd
4 Fitzhardinge Street
London W1H 0AH

Contents

Acknowledgment

I have had the good fortune to receive generous help from many quarters: Dr Aileen Ribeiro and Mrs Stella Mary Newton did much to encourage my interest in the history of dress both at the Courtauld Institute and in researching this book, and I received prompt help and attention from the Publisher, and more particularly Mrs Belinda Baker and Miss Rachel Wright. I should also like to thank Miss Wendy Hefford of the Victoria & Albert Museum for her kindness in discussing with me shawls in her care and for directing my attention to further areas for study; Noreen and Jack Brennan, who provided invaluable help in reading parts of the text and in dealing with the Frick Collection in New York on my behalf; Michael Dillon for taking so much trouble to lend me materials that I had found difficult to procure; my brother, Charles McKay, for sending me so many useful books from the States (and the apt gift of a shawl); the curators and staff of many museums and photographic collections who took considerable trouble to help my work; Miss Mary Bennett of the Walker Art Gallery, Liverpool; Miss Penelope Byrde of the Museum of Costume, Bath; Mr R.P. Caldicott of the Worthing Borough Council; Miss Pamela Clabburn; Mr Peter Day of Chatsworth; Miss Rosemary Evison of the National Portrait Gallery; Mr Jeremy Farrell of the Museum of Costume and Textiles, Nottingham; Mme Marie-Dominique Frieh of the Musée Historique des Tissus, Lyons; Miss Theresa-Mary Morton of The Royal Library, Windsor Castle; Miss Veronica Murphy of the Victoria & Albert Museum; Mrs Valerie Reilly of the Paisley Museum and Art Galleries; Miss Carol Sacha of the Farnham Museum; Miss Fiona Strodder of Strangers Hall Museum, Norwich; Miss Jane Tozer of the Gallery of English Costume, Platt Hall; and Mrs Elizabeth Wright of the National Museum of Antiquities of Scotland. I owe my greatest thanks to my husband, John, for all his help in the writing of this work and for taking some of the photographs (numbers 2, 21, 59, 63, 68, 70, 76 and colour plates 3, 6, 7 and 8). Without his guidance and inspiration the book would never have been completed.

List of Illustrations

69 Hermine Gallia, by Gustav Klimt, 1904 (*National Gallery, London*).

70 Fashion plate from the *Journal des Dames et des Modes,* 1912, (from Fashion in Paris from the 'Journal des Dames et des Modes' 1912–1913, *Thames and Hudson*).

71 'Smart Boas for Spring Wear', advertisement by Messrs Swan and Edgar Ltd, 1916 (*B.T. Batsford*).

72 Indian shawl, *c.* 1900 (*Worthing Museum and Art Gallery*).

73 Black net shawl, *c.* 1910–20 (*Worthing Museum and Art Gallery*).

74 Black silk crêpe shawl, *c.* 1920–30 (*Worthing Museum and Art Gallery*).

75 Fashion photograph of a peasant shawl, designed by Frank Usher, 1972 (*Frank Usher*).

76 Cover from *Vogue*, 1 July 1918 (*author's collection*).

77 Design for a scarf, by Raoul Dufy, *c.* 1928 (*Witt Library, Courtauld Institute of Art, London and Bianchini Férier, Lyons*).

78 Advertisement for Mayfair scarves, September 1944 (*B.T. Batsford*).

1   King Ashurnasirpal II of Assyria, 883–859 BC, attired
for religious ceremonies. His shawl is folded lengthwise
in two to display the fringed ends above each other,
while being wound about the body to form a kind of
skirt.

2   Fashion plate from the Journal des Dames et des
Modes, 25 February 1798. Founded during the
preceding year, La Mésangère's periodical is an
invaluable source for contemporary French fashions,
while the editor was always alert to English influences.

Introduction

Material has been draped over the head or around the neck, to fall gracefully over shoulders and chest, in both East and West from very early times. Although the focus of this book is the period from the seventeenth century to the early 1980s, the past, and more especially antiquity, has often exerted a powerful influence on later fashions. While nearly three millennia separate King Ashurnasirpal II of Assyria from this *élégante* of 1798, their stole-like shawls are quite similar, especially in the way they are worn. Both are woollen, secured at the waist, and draped over the left shoulder, with the long fringed ends tiered one above the other. The resemblance between the two fashions is so striking as to arouse the suspicion that the fashionable lady of the French Directory has modelled her attire on the dress of the Assyrians. That was far from impossible, as a relief very similar to the one illustrated here was lodged in the Louvre, which had just been opened to the public as France's first national museum. Furthermore, Pierre de La Mésangère, the editor of the journal in which the fashion plate of the *élégante* appears frequently exhorted artists to study the dress of antiquity from the statues in the Louvre.[1] Even in later periods, when the moulders of fashion appear to have been oblivious of the past, they often fell unawares beneath the influence of earlier fashions.

The two illustrations also demonstrate the accessory's remarkable versatility. It could, as here, combine the properties of both shawl and stole by covering the shoulders and hanging as a narrow strip of material to one side of the body. On other occasions the accessory would shrink to the proportions of a scarf that might be worn as a sash, as was common in the seventeenth century, or tied around the neck, as is usual today. Shawls, stoles and scarves: the attraction of these accessories lies in the ambiguity with which the boundaries are drawn between them. It is precisely the mercurial way in which they are apt to merge into one another, that makes it so desirable to treat all three within the confines of a single study.

Shawls, stoles and scarves stand out among accessories by achieving their effect at least as much by

the style in which they are worn, as by their own characteristics. Shawls and long scarves, in particular, seem to speak for the wearer's whole personality. Change that part of the wearer's silhouette, and her whole character is altered so that she becomes barely recognizable. Nothing proves this point so well as the accessory's fascination for actresses since at least the eighteenth century. It was Lady Hamilton's remarkable shawl dances which enthralled Goethe and a whole generation, and which first brought home the garment's protean qualities to the fashionable world at the end of the eighteenth century (see fig. 29). Since that time many others have donned the shawl in one of its forms to cast their own very personal spell: Isadora Duncan as she danced in the swirling beauty of her long silk scarves, by one of which she was all too aptly strangled in a tragic car accident; the dancers in the *Ballet Russe* who often used shawls and scarves to help create their mesmeric effect; and those who wore the long white fox stoles designed by Paul Poiret, who drew much of his inspiration from the same ballet.

Although fashion rings the changes on shawls, stoles and scarves throughout the ages, each has always retained its own distinctive attractions, while at any particular time one of the three has usually achieved ascendancy over the others. In antiquity, the shawl reigned almost unchallenged. Hence its appeal at the end of the eighteenth century when Europe turned to 'the Antique' for inspiration. It was the Romantics in the following century, however, who prized the shawl above any other accessory, presumably for the way in which it frames the heart and magically transforms the wearer. As for the stole, since at least the time of the Assyrians it has remained an ecclesiastical garment. The stole-like pallium for much of the Middle Ages served as the badge of primacy, conferred traditionally by the Pope on metropolitans and archbishops. At the time of the French Revolution the stole was still commonly used to symbolize the clerical estate, and indeed continues to be used by priests to this day. Yet it is by no means the first garment charged with religious significance that fashionable ladies have presumed to appropriate, and the pious may well be wondering uneasily what they will dare to purloin next! Finally, the scarf has hardly ever lacked a following, at least in modern times. It has often proved invaluable to fashionable ladies for the way it may be used to lend a suggestion of modesty to a *décolletage* while actually enhancing its attractions.

Perhaps in these more uninhibited times the scarf would have gone into eclipse, if it had not received support from an unexpected quarter. Her Majesty Queen Elizabeth II, by donning a headscarf on informal occasions, has persuaded a few fashionable ladies and many others to follow her example.

1

The Inventive Century
1600 –1700

Seventeenth-century men and women experimented with a bewildering range of shapes and styles for scarves and stoles. The first impression of the century's dress is apt to be of a restless search for novelty, of change for the sake of change itself. On closer acquaintance, what stands out is the ability of people in the period to absorb diverse influences and to bring them together harmoniously. For, by about 1700, a single style, enriched by borrowings from the Renaissance, the Orient and military dress, was coming into being. There were few major developments in shawls, scarves and stoles – the eighteenth-century revival of the Antique being a notable exception – that cannot be traced back to the inventive seventeenth century.

BORROWINGS FROM THE RENAISSANCE

Scarves had tended to dwindle in size during the Renaissance. Pietro Lorenzetti's fresco in the Opera del Duomo, Siena, known as *The Birth of the Virgin* (1342) during the early Renaissance, shows her wearing a long scarf, in general appearance not unlike the shawls of the late eighteenth century. Well before the seventeenth century, scarves were little more than wispy frills around the neck, designed as token relief from the severity of the starched ruffs that dominate the portraits of the time. In Pershore Abbey there is a tomb surmounted by an effigy, dating from 1600–1615, where the ladies wear scarves of this sort, just visible above their ruffs and crossed in front of the bodices.

3   Figures from the Haselwood Tomb, Pershore Abbey, 1600–1615. Small, narrow scarves of cloth or silk worn around the neck and bodice were very common and date back to the reign of Elizabeth I.

4   *Lady Catherine Howard by John Hoskins, c. 1649.*
Her bare bosom and shoulders are partly covered by
the edge of the lace chemisette and scarf.

The neckerchief was another style popular in the first half of the seventeenth century. A large linen square, either plain, as was common in New England, or edged with lace, was folded diagonally and worn around the shoulders like a small shawl. The fashion could be varied agreeably by fastening the neckerchief at either throat or breast, or by just allowing it to fall free.[1] A finely drawn example of one in 1643 can be seen in Wenceslaus Hollar's 'Winter', to be discussed later in connection with the magnificent fur tippet worn over the neckerchief (see fig. 6).

The fashion for expansive *décolletage* at the court of Charles I led to the use of long silk scarves in colours or tones to contrast with that of the bodice. The scarves were sometimes of satin, as can be seen in the miniature of Lady Catherine Howard painted by John Hoskins about 1649. The scarf, as depicted here, adds an attractive informality by the casual way it is draped across the left shoulder to contrast with the rather formal cut of the dress.

The head rail was another fashion inherited from the sixteenth century, and one which went right back to the Middle Ages. As can be seen from a brass of 1632 in the Church of St Mary, Stoke-by-Nayland, Suffolk (fig. 5), the head rail was so capacious that it resembled a shawl in the way it covered the top of the head and the shoulders partially as well, before reaching almost to the ground behind. Any suspicion that the head rail might be atypical of the period is belied by the very fashionable character of the bodice and the 'balloon' sleeves. Nonetheless, its association with the past was probably the reason why the head rail was abandoned shortly afterwards, and had to await revival in the nineteenth century, when the Romantics prized it precisely for its medieval character.

The seventeenth century inherited from its predecessor a kind of stole called a tippet, which was derived from the original medieval cote-hardie. In the sixteenth-century version the simplified cape usually retained the original pendant streamers, often of fur. A striking feature of this accessory was the way the animal's head was sometimes framed with jewels and precious metals.[2] Although tippets are seldom mentioned in the seventeenth century, to judge by Lady Verney's letter to her husband in 1639 concerning the portrait which she had just commissioned, they were much prized in high society. 'Put Sr. Vandyke in remembrance to do my picture wel', she ordered. 'I have some sables with the clasp of them set with dimons – if thos that I am pictuerde in were don so, I think it would look very well in the picture.'[3] For an example of a tippet in England of the mid-seventeenth century, it would be hard to overlook the claims of Wenceslaus Hollar. He had already established his reputation as an etcher of small genre scenes in Cologne and elsewhere, when he was engaged in 1636 by the second Earl of Arundel to depict the places that he visited on his mission to the Emperor. On joining the Arundel household in England, he chose to specialize in the rendering of women's dress.[4] The striking view of 'Winter' in 1643 from his *Four Seasons* (fig. 6), shows the voluminous furs of the period, and notably the tippet and muff at their most luxurious. The seasons are probably based on the wardrobe of the Countess. For that reason, these garments, although undoubtedly fashionable, may well have been closer to the Dutch style of the old court than to the French style affected by the court of Charles I, from which the Countess kept aloof.[5]

In the 1670s the fur tippet reappeared at the court of Louis XIV, which as the main centre of European fashion seems to have promoted its adoption elsewhere. The accessory was brought to the French court by Liselotte von der Pfalz – hence the name 'palatine' – when she married Philippe d'Orléans, the brother of Louis XIV. The palatine's chief function in Eastern Europe, as it had doubtless earlier been in the West, was proclaimed in its other German name, *Flohpelzchen*. These 'flea cravats' were prized by the wearers as a useful means of disposing of vermin, which could be collected in the fur and shaken out, doubtless more often than not on to innocent bystanders. The *Flohpelzchen* was particularly in demand at the Habsburg court, as the strict etiquette there forbade scratching in public. As the Princess relates in her amusing letters, when she first wore it in

---

5 Dorothy, Lady Mannock, 1632. Her long head rail is shaped by cutting one corner straight across and turning it back. This part was then pinned on to the back of the hair to allow the entire head rail to cascade down the back of her fashionable dress.

1671 she was subjected to so much ridicule that she scarcely dared wear what she called her *zibeline*. Five years later it was a very different matter. Admitted to the King's private circle, largely on the strength of her witty conversation, Liselotte von der Pfalz found that the despised *zibeline* or palatine was being copied on all sides by obsequious courtiers and had become highly fashionable.[6]

MILITARY SASHES AND CRAVATS

Military uniforms may seem an unpromising source for innovations in dress. Are uniforms not intended by their very nature to impose society's will upon individuals? That was, perhaps, an important part of their attraction, alongside their novelty in the seventeenth century. Even at the Battle of Warsaw in 1651 the Brandenburgers and

R. Gaywood fecit

4

6 'Winter' from The Four Seasons, by Wenceslaus Hollar, 1643. Among the fashionable accessories worn by this English lady are a linen neckerchief edged with lace over her low-cut bodice, a black hood and linen coif over her head, and a sable tippet and matching muff.

Swedes wore no uniforms, and were distinguishable from each other by only the most rudimentary, not to say bucolic, insignia: the Brandenburgers attached small branches of oak tree to their hats, while the Swedes made do with a handful of straw. The beginnings of proper uniforms in modern times for whole armies, and even regiments, were the coloured sashes which came to be worn about the time of the Thirty Years War. Thus at the Battle of Lüten (1632) the Imperial troops wore red

7 Edward Sackville, Fourth Earl of Dorset (d. 1652), by John Hoskins. This miniature betrays the influence of military dress on fashionable, although the sash has become purely decorative.

sashes and the Swedes green.[7] Yet, although military uniforms were slow to be brought into use, by about the turn of the century they were coming increasingly to symbolize the might of the state and to confer at least on the officers, both in the armed forces and in the civil administration, something of the prestige of the modern state.

The sash worn crosswise across the trunk had a long pedigree. Early in the century it was still a sort of haverstock, running from hip to opposite shoulder, in which provisions could be carried. That use showed its

8 Paola Adorna, Marchesa di Brignole-Sale, by Sir Anthony van Dyck, c. 1622–27. Women, too, wore sashes, often made entirely of precious jewels, and arranged baldric-wise across their sharply pointed stomachers.

affinity with the so-called 'scarf' of the Middle Ages, which was a kind of satchel worn over the shoulder. The use of the sash as distinctive insignia to indicate either allegiance or rank was the all-important *point de départ* of the modern uniform. Sashes around the time of the English Civil War (1642–7) still seem to have been quite simple. Edward Sackville, Fourth Earl of Dorset (died 1652), in the fine portrait of him by John Hoskins (fig. 7),

wears a blue silk sash that measures about four inches across, and which runs from his right shoulder to emerge from beneath his wide lace collar and pass across his chest to waist level. King Charles I himself wore just such a simple sash baldric-wise in his portrait painted by Daniel Mytens in 1631 (located in the National Portrait Gallery, London). So, surprisingly, did women. Paola Adorna, Marchesa di Brignole-Sale, in the portrait painted by Sir Anthony van Dyck, wore one as early as 1622–7 (fig. 8).

By the 1670s sashes had become a very prominent item of civil attire, as can be seen in the engraving in fig. 9 of J.D. de St Jean's *Man of Quality in Winter Clothing*. The enormous width and elaborate style of the fur and heavily embroidered lengthwise sash might seem to border on caricature, were it not for the artist's reputation as one of the most reliable depictors of the period's fashions. Besides, the Crown itself would not have authenticated the print with its seal of approval – *privilège du Roy* – if the dress, so essential to the maintenance of the social hierarchy, had been rendered inaccurately. The fact that the print is dated precisely, 1678, and openly advertised as being on sale *aux deux globes* on the *quai des grands augustins*, also lends it credibility. If further proof is needed, it is only necessary to visit *Le Magasin des Modes*, engraved by Jean Bérain in the same year. Not only does the fashionable man in the shop wear a similar sash, but others are prominently displayed for sale behind him. As for the shop itself, it looks as if it might well be situated in the Palais Royal. In any case, the fashions have been observed closely, as the print appears in the *Mercure Galant*, which was prized by its readers for its advice on dress; indeed, the periodical often went so far as to recommend particular costumiers, to whom it looked for financial support.[8]

The cravat was also of military origin. In the first instance, it is supposed to have been worn by Roman soldiers. Its reintroduction at the end of the seventeenth century was ascribed by contemporaries to the Croatian Regiment of Louis XIV. That certainly fits the date of its appearance around 1678, and the corruption of *croate* into *cravate* would surely rank as the merest peccadillo in the history of linguistics. At that time the cravat was a length of white linen with a section of lace at each end.[9]

As early as the 1680s the cravat was sufficiently established to be used itself as a vehicle for sartorial

◁ *9* Man of Quality in Winter Clothing, *by J.D. de St Jean, 1678. The back view shows the long line of the collarless justaucorps with the skirts flaring out slightly from the low waistline. The highly ornate stole-like sash is held in place by a wide scarf.*

10 Le Magasin des Modes, *by Jean Bérain, 1678. The fashionable frequented such boutiques, often to be found at the Palais Royal in Paris. It is interesting to see ready-made sashes and cravats with their strings in bows (on the left), and scarves, like the one the lady is wearing on the right, at such an early date.*

innovation. Antoine Trouvain, one of the period's ablest recorders of dress, captured the raffish appearance of the chevalier de Bouillon in 1684. (The print is located in the Pierpont Morgan Library in New York.) The vast expanse of the chevalier's shirt was partially filled by his unusually long and pleated oval cravat. Although styles would vary, large cravats soon became fashionable, probably because they were one answer to the problem of covering the large area of shirt front then commonly

11 Madame de Ludre en Steinkerke et Falbala, *by N.* ▷ *Arnoult, 1692. The still lines of the fontange head-dress and tight bodice are relieved by the Steinkirk cravat, which is draped loosely around the neck to be pinned in a loop on the right, in the fashionable style.*

exhibited. That display by the fashionable was practically *de rigueur*, because those who buttoned up their coats tightly were accused of trying to hide dirty linen. Another remarkable feature of the chevalier's dress is the shawl collar, usually associated with the nineteenth century, although many examples can be found in the portraits of Holbein in the sixteenth century.

Soldiers not only invented the accessory, they also set the fashion for the style in which it was worn. The Steinkirk cravat is thought to have taken its name from the famous battle of 1692, when French soldiers, surprised by the enemy, hurriedly stuffed their cravats through a buttonhole in their coats to be ready to face their opponents. The impromptu act of heroes was echoed almost instantly in the studied negligence of the fashionable for almost forty years. The only noticeable variation was that the long cravat, usually edged resplendently with lace and knotted loosely under the chin, might sometimes be pinned to one side instead of being threaded through a buttonhole.[10] Again, women appropriated the fashion for themselves with astonishing speed. In the year of the battle, a singer at the opera in Paris, Mlle Le Rochois, appeared in one of her roles with a lace cravat thrown negligently over her coat. The print of *Madame de Ludre en Stenkerke et Falbala* (fig. 11) is actually dated the year of the battle, a quite remarkable achievement, especially as a print of this sort would have taken several months to produce by the methods in use at the time.

ORIENTAL INFLUENCES
The Orient fascinated English society in the seventeenth century to the extent that almost every wardrobe reflected its influence, while King Charles II himself appears to have looked to Persia for a model on which to base his Utopian project for an unchanging court dress. Inspiration seems to have come in the first place from travellers' accounts, nearly all of which provided detailed descriptions of oriental costumes. It was the visit of the English Embassy to the Great Mogul in 1622 that really seems to have fired society's imagination. A very informative account by the Embassy's chaplain, Edward Terry, appeared in 1655, a delay of over thirty years since the original expedition which in itself seems to indicate continued public interest in it. Republication in 1777 seems to show that Terry's work had achieved the standing of a classic.[11]

The portrait of Samuel Pepys by John Hayls shows just how fashionable oriental costume had become by 1666. Pepys himself was a top civil servant who worked in close collaboration with Charles II on the administration of the Navy. The caution instilled by his calling was reinforced by his personality: it is well known that Pepys

always strove to be 'correct' in dress and behaviour.[12] It seems significant, therefore, that he chose to be painted in this informal, but highly fashionable, attire. The salient feature of his dress is the golden-brown silk gown, which, he confides to the reader of his *Diary*, 'I hired to be drawn in; an Indian gowne, and I do see also the reason to expect a most excellent picture of it.'[13] The choice of the gown is all the more significant because of the trouble he took to rent one, although he had bought one himself some five years earlier.[14] Clearly, he considered the hired garment the last word in fashion, and may also have relished its associations with intellectuals and artists. Pepys himself is shown holding a sheet of music, and it may also be significant that Isaac Newton and John Locke were portrayed in rather similar gowns.

As for the Indian gown itself, it appears to have been introduced around 1634, when a correspondent from Amsterdam wrote ruefully, 'I have just now undone myself with buying an Indian warme gowne.' In the course of time, as Margaret Swain notes in a most illuminating article (see Bibliography), the so-called Indian gown was also made in Europe and not necessarily even from Indian material. What was prized primarily was the garment's oriental appearance. Its high cost, to which the letter-writer of 1634 referred, and borne out also by Pepys's decision to hire an Indian gown for his portrait, suggests that it played an important part in pioneering the fashionable negligence affected at the time. The Indian gown, therefore, seems quite distinct in appearance and function from its predecessor, the nightgown. The latter dated back to the sixteenth century and was still worn in the early seventeenth century. 'It was warm and might be trimmed, or lined with fur, and had long set-in sleeves, often slit', notes Margaret Swain.[15] The nightgown was designed for casual indoor attire in the daytime – the word nightgown itself being quite distinct from present-day usage – after sword, coat and wig had been discarded. In social terms, the main difference was that the nightgown was not worn in company, while the Indian gown was the *dernier cri* among the fashionable.

As can be seen from Pepys's portrait, the Indian gown was very loose-fitting, with long simple sleeves and without lapels. It made an admirable accompaniment to the simple white knotted neckcloth and floppy shirt

12 Samuel Pepys, by John Hayls, 1666. The diarist is ▷ *shown in the period's highly fashionable informality, achieved by wearing an Indian gown (especially hired) and a plain, loosely knotted neckcloth.*

sleeves. The diarist's debonair attire was completed by the sash tied around his waist and just visible behind his elbow.

The Indian gown was to remain fashionable, indeed, was to increase in appeal in the eighteenth century, in the new version called the banyan. It was, however, always to remain obdurately informal. The matter was put to the test by none other than the King himself in October 1666. Charles II had declared, according to Evelyn, that he would 'leave the French mode, which had hitherto obtain'd to our great expence and reproch'. In its place he resolved to 'put himself solemnly into the eastern fashion of vest, changeing doublet, stiff collar, bands and cloake, into a comely dress, after ye Persian mode, . . . resolving never to alter it'. Predictably enough, the courtiers who bet the King that he would fail in his attempt to stem the tide of fashion were right. Yet, as Barbara Baines shows in her delightful *Fashion Revivals*, the Orient continued to fascinate the British, especially Londoners, for whom ambassadors from the East staged many displays of their lands' exotic costumes.[16] It was hardly surprising, therefore, that interest in the Orient during the eighteenth century was to border on obsession.

Another accessory that may have drawn its inspiration from the East was the Spanish mantilla, which dated from the sixteenth century. It is described by François Boucher as a 'reduced version of the old *manto* or cape, worn indoor and out, recalling oriental styles'. It was always made of light material and covered only head, neck and shoulders; it seems to have been far more attractive than the voluminous heavy *manto* it replaced. That garment was, in effect, a heavy shawl, worn by widows and young girls, who were allowed to show only one eye – which restriction must, indeed, have set a premium on enterprise among ladies in the sixteenth century.[17] Judging from the way the sitter, in the fine portrait of *Lady in a Mantilla* by Velázquez about 1625–30, charmingly holds the right end of her mantilla, the practice of covering one eye, for whatever reason, may even have continued into the seventeenth century! The mantilla with its beautiful black lace, set off by the white collar in the portrait, would, perhaps, be Spain's most prized fashion accessory over the centuries, and will reappear in successive chapters.

13 Lady in a Mantilla, *by Velázquez, c. 1625–30. The ▷ mantilla lent informality to the stiff Spanish silhouette. Black silk lace mantillas, with their bold floral designs, were to retain their appeal for centuries, and were to be adopted in nineteenth-century England.*

2
From the 'Modest' Scarf to the 'Antique' Shawl
1700–1800

Fashion for most of the century was a battlefield between the oriental and the Antique. It was only in the 1790s that the two sometimes fused together in a magnificent union of opposites.

THE 'MODEST' SCARF

The scarf might be described as the unsung heroine of accessories: found everywhere, it is seldom noticed, yet is an essential constituent in many of the century's fashions. It served styles derived from both the Orient and the Antique, a peace-keeping role for which it received scant recognition. The scarf was also often 'modest' in another sense, which doubtless gained it more appreciation, until rudely supplanted by the shawl, a kind of outgrown scarf, from about the 1780s. For the scarf often proved indispensable in lending an air of modesty to a *décolletage*, which it actually set off.

Scarves were used in a bewildering variety of ways in the early eighteenth century. In the absence of any clearly marked developments, the influence of the preceding century remained strong. The most popular legacy among the well-to-do was probably the Steinkirk cravat, discussed in the previous chapter. Thus Lady Easy in Colley Cibber's *The Careless Husband* of 1704 'takes a Steinkirk off her neck'.[1] Men, so often more conservative in matters of dress, bore the Steinkirk with heroic determination for a further seventy years. Although decidedly in eclipse after 1730, it was still being sported in David Garrick's *Bon Ton* of 1775, where an old gentleman is described with 'one of the knots of his tie hanging down his left shoulder, and his fringed cravat nicely twisted down his breast and thrust through his gold button-hole'.[2] Despite Garrick's mockery, a not-dissimilar cravat gained notoriety, if not acceptance, by the social élite, when it was pioneered by the macaronis around 1777. 'The Macaroni Cravat', according to the Cunningtons, 'was also made of muslin edged with lace and usually tied with a bow under the chin, the ends dangling', as was sometimes the case with the Steinkirk itself.[3]

The designers of men's neckwear were perhaps shown at their most inventive by the solitaire. This item,

which flourished between the 1730s and the 1770s, was a thin black tie worn over a stock. It was almost always attached to a bag wig behind, and arranged in front in a variety of ingenious ways. At its simplest and most attractive the solitaire was a narrow ribbon encircling the neck, rather in the manner that certain orders are still worn today. Another version was worn round the neck in a narrow tight black band, reminiscent of a lady's choker, or a dog-collar, and, indeed, one worn by dogs rather than clergymen. A style that seems to have been particularly fashionable was to tie the ends in a large bow-tie, on which the chin might appear to rest, as the neck was sandwiched between the tie in front and the bag wig behind (which was itself sometimes formed to look like a bow-tie).[4]

By about 1735 the stock was beginning to oust the cravat. It has been well described as 'a piece of linen or cambric folded to form a high neckband and sometimes stiffened with pasteboard'.[5] The stock was always white, except that the black military stock was affected by sporting bucks. As the century progressed, the stock steadily mounted the wearer's neck until it reached once more the proportions of a full-blown cravat. Before that point was reached, however, the stock was reinforced with pasteboard, which could occasion the wearer discomfort practically to the point of making him a martyr to fashion. 'My neck is stretched out in such a manner that I am apprehensive of having my throat cut with the pasteboard', lamented a correspondent to the *Gentleman's Magazine* in 1761.[6]

Some, however, might have found that end preferable to wearing the Directory cravat which was to come. Many contemporaries observed that the way it covered the chin and threatened to engulf the ears, gave France the appearance of a country struck by an epidemic of goitre which the cravat was designed to mask. *Les Payables*, of 1797, depicts just such a cravat on the central figure, who is unmistakably an *incroyable*. His wide-striped lapels, boots and close-fitting breeches, which almost resemble today's tights, are all in character. It is, however, the full Directory cravat that shows him to be dressed in the height of fashion. The

accessory was so much admired that the lady on his left seems to believe, perhaps mistakenly, that it would look as well on a woman as on a man.

As *Les Payables* is transparently a caricature, can it be taken as a guide to the appearance of the Directory cravat? The cravat and other features are, in fact, echoed in many contemporary prints, notably those by Debucourt and Boilly, both perceptive depictors of the dress of their times. Yet, if these are *incroyables* and *merveilleuses* (the name usually given to the partners of the former), are they representative of high society? On the evidence of prints such a Chataignier's *Reception of the Directors*, the *incroyables* were, in effect, the leaders of fashion, even if some of their more daring vestimentary sallies were toned down by the more mature members of the social élite. Yet, it is clear from *Le Petit Coblentz* of Isabey, an artistic observer of impeccable reliability, that even the royalist opponents of the régime adopted its fashions, and more especially the voluminous cravat. In any case, the ultimate accolade of sartorial approval was conferred by the Prince Regent's arbiter of elegance, Beau Brummell himself. He can be observed in John Cook's portrait of about 1798

14 Les Payables, anonymous engraving of 1797. The incroyable wears a cravat that threatens to engulf his ears and chin. The 'scrofulous', as it was called, was a large square of silk or muslin (sometimes edged with lace), folded into a triangle, wrapped around the neck twice and knotted with a bow in front. Like the Steinkirk, it was also adopted by women.

wearing one of his famous cravats (fig. 15). Such was the perfection that the Prince Regent admired, and sought in vain to copy by visiting Beau Brummell with the specific intention of watching the master fold and tie his cravat. In the eyes of the Regency bucks these cravats were the summit of the century's achievements. That, however, was a claim that their womenfolk would not allow to go unchallenged.

Women in the early eighteenth century wore their scarves with an inventive grace unequalled by their menfolk. The scarf which was worn most, up till about 1740, dated from the preceding century. It has been described as 'a large wrap enveloping the body,

Scarves were sometimes used instead of ribbons to secure hats, by tying them from crown to chin. This practice was particularly common with the large straw hats at the end of the century which could easily be caught by the wind. Fulfilling much the same function were lappets, which were long streamers, usually one on each side, hanging down to keep the hat in place. They were particularly common with the flimsy mob caps so often worn throughout the century for informal attire, and quite often worn on other occasions under sturdier and more formal headgear.

'The new thing called a scarf, with its depending tassels, looks so much like an advertisement that if the place of abode were added, there is no doubt but that it

15 Beau Brummell, by John Cook, c. 1798. His cravat 'was worn without stiffening of any kind, and bagged out in front, ruching up to the chin in a roll; to remedy this obvious awkwardness and inconvenience, he used to have his slightly starched, and a reasoning mind must allow that there is not much to object to in this reform'. (Captain Jesse, The Life of George Brummell.)

16 Dame Mary Pettus, anonymous artist, c. 1740–50. Her wrapping gown has a close-fitted bodice with a low décolletage and without robings. It was usual, as here, for propriety's sake to insert a tucker and modesty piece.

rounded in shape and falling to waist level behind and lower in front'. Some were so voluminous that they even had sleeves. As for materials, they ran from velvet to silk or gauze. The scarves were frequently trimmed with furbelows, especially between 1700 and 1715, or with flounces or scalloped borders.[7]

The tucker, which can be traced back to at least 1688, was in vogue especially between 1730 and 1750, and continued to the end of the century. It can really be classed as a kind of scarf, and is described by the Cunningtons as 'a white frilled edging to the low-necked bodices, and very common with closed robes. It arose from the day shift or was sewn on separately and edged with lace'. It was often worn in conjunction with the modesty piece, which covered 'the pit of the bosom'.[8] Examples of both can be seen in the portrait of Dame Mary Pettus (fig. 16).

would draw in custom.' (*London Magazine*, July 1766.)[9] What was this 'new thing called a scarf'? It cannot have been the accessory itself, which had been in use for centuries, as we have seen. As for the term 'scarf', that too appears to have been well established in its modern sense by the beginning of the eighteenth century. As early as 1710 Swift was boasting in his *Journal to Stella* that he had commissioned not one, but two ladies to procure him scarves.[10] (His motive, of course, was not that the accessory was in short supply, but only the time-honoured appeal to women to aid the helpless male.) Two years later the *Spectator* mentions a 'scarf', as if the word were familiar to its readers.[11] So, 'the new thing called a scarf' appears in reality to have been a new use for something old. And, indeed, by the 1760s and even earlier, the scarf had begun to play a far more significant role in women's dress. The scarf, or handkerchief, as it was often called, was then being draped around the *décolletage*, brought to a V in front, sometimes pinned behind, or the ends tucked into the bosom, or left to fall in front of the stomacher, where it was secured by ribbons.[12] In a period when ankles were hidden discreetly beneath skirts, the main focus of erotic interest in polite society was naturally the bosom. The scarf, as the accessory most intimately associated with it, therefore, enjoyed a privileged position in the fashions of the time.

To appreciate just how far scarves were integrated in contemporary fashions, it is only necessary to examine their designs. In the 1760s there were two rival styles, the Rococo and the Antique. Both held sway over all areas of taste, but more especially interior decoration, of which women in fashionable dress were regarded as a part, alongside the crystal chandeliers and the Meissen porcelain. From this masculine world women would certainly have been banished if their dresses had not echoed the motifs around them. A scarf might have been deemed too unimportant for regulation. Yet, in practice, as a fine example at the Metropolitan Museum of Art in New York shows, an eighteenth-century lady could be Rococo right down to her scarf, of which one was described in a recent exhibition: 'White silk trimmed with green and pink silk flowers alternating with rocaille shapes in silver thread; edged with silver lace. French, about 1760.'[13]

Greek taste is all the rage; our furniture, our jewellery, Material, hair-style, carriage. Everything is Greek except our souls.[14]

This was a typical comment in a light comedy of 1764. Baron Grimm, who had set himself up as a kind of arbiter of elegance for crowned heads in his *Correspondance Littéraire*, had already declared: 'During the last few years we have favoured shapes and ornaments in the antique style. This represents a great advance in taste and fashion and now has so many advocates that everything in Paris today has to be *à la grecque*.'[15] It is fascinating to observe, in the very imaginatively chosen illustrations of Svend Eriksen's *Early Neo-classicism in France*, how often the same motif appears in furniture and dress fabrics alike. And the requirement for the fashionable lady to dress *à la grecque* applied demonstrably to scarves, as well as to other items of dress. In a *Portrait of an Unknown Lady* by Alexandre Roslin in 1766, a scarf bears the unmistakable Grecian key design, which in turn is remarkably similar to the carving on the armchair in P.-A. Baudoin's engraving, *Le Lever* of 1765.[16]

From the Antique to Nature was a short, but nonetheless decisive, step. Its hallmark of the 1780s was the *buffon*, known somewhat indelicately as 'the pouter-pigeon effect', achieved by compressing the waist and thrusting forward the bosom. As this posture was, in reality, highly unnatural and most uncomfortable, a scarf was artfully used to help create the illusion of a distended breast, whilst seeming to disown the strain necessary to achieve it with the loose informality of the scarf itself. The *buffon* is seen at its most enchanting in Gainsborough's magnificent painting, *The Morning Walk*, of 1785. Mrs Hallett wears a very plain open robe of light white silk, set off by a black sash around her waist. The dress itself is topped with a muslin *buffon*, tied with a ribbon bow. The contrived carelessness of her ensemble is completed by the soft silk gauze stole, clinging loosely to her arm. It is interesting to observe how much of the wonderfully ethereal effect has been achieved by the two scarves, and especially by the remarkable long diaphanous stole, although many dress historians seem oblivious of its existence at this period. Yet, as Dr Aileen Ribeiro has pointed out, 'this familiar portrait expressed the ideal of English fashionable dress in the 1780s, which was followed all over Europe'.[17]

The *buffon*'s coquettish possibilities were too tempting for the style not to be abused. Scarves mounted unchecked practically to engulf the chin and almost the entire face. 'Ladies with neckerchiefs puffed up so high

17 Mr and Mrs Hallett, from The Morning Walk *by* ▷ *Thomas Gainsborough, 1785. In Mrs Hallett's dress the severity of the neo-classical chemise has given way to a Romantic look where the fine muslin* buffon, *transparent gauze silk stole, shimmering silk skirt and waving plumes create an illusion of wafted movement.*

18 *Fashion plate from the* Journal de la Mode et du Goût, *25 February 1790. The white skirt with blue border, tight-fitting caraco in blue-and-white-striped satin, patterned* mouchoir anglais, *echoing the colours of skirt and caraco, billowing white gauze fichu menteur, felt hat trimmed with silver and surmounted by an aigrette, are all typical of the opulent dress early in the French Revolution.*

their noses were scarcely visible', noted the author of *Sophie in London* in 1786. And again in the *Ipswich Journal* for 1787, 'a large bouffant of white gauze carried up near the chin'.[18] The most elaborate effects were often achieved with the help of starch.[19] The intention remained as transparent as some of the period's light muslin dresses themselves, and is well conveyed in the rather ungallant French expression, *fichu menteur*, or fibbing scarf, designed to create the illusion that the lady was more generously endowed around the bust than was actually the case. While the fashion's immediate appeal was frankly erotic, it also had a profound effect in altering the whole feminine silhouette. When ladies from about 1789 went around enveloped in fichus puffed up to their chins, placed less emphasis on wide hips, and wore high cylindrical hats, they looked considerably taller.[20] In that sense, the neo-classical look which was now emerging created a new woman, elongated, slender and sometimes athletic – a very different being from the delicate Rococo lady whom she had replaced. To say that 'it was all done by scarves' (and shawls, to be considered shortly) may be an exaggeration, but is not far from the truth.

Did the Romantics issue from, or develop as a reaction against, the Antique? Such an unanswerable question is best left to art historians. Nonetheless, it is worth bearing it in mind while examining Elisabeth Vigée-Lebrun's *Self-Portrait* of 1790 (see colour plate 2). 'I used to twist a *fichu de mousseline* around the head, as you can see from my portraits in Florence and at St Petersburg.'[21] This would have had little influence, had she not been one of France's most fashionable portraitists. In a recent exhibition it can be seen that several of her sitters followed her example.[22] Mme Vigée-Lebrun was in any case something of an aspirant *couturière*. In her *Souvenirs* she boasted:

> As I was horrified by the dress which women wore then [before the Revolution], I devoted all my efforts to making it a little more picturesque. I was overjoyed when I won the confidence of my sitters, to clothe them as I wished. Shawls were not yet being worn, but I used to arrange large scarves loosely interlaced around their bodies and over their arms. In that way I tried to imitate the beautiful draped style of Raphael and Domenichino.[23]

It is interesting to note that, in the view of this experienced painter, it was the positioning of the scarves, more than anything else, that transformed the appearance of the sitter.

To return to the portrait, what is so riveting about the painter's appearance? The headscarf may well look familiar because turbans had been a favourite fashion

accessory since at least the opening years of the century. Perhaps the novelty of the head-dress lies in its faintly Byronic character. The muslin scarf, ruffled around the artist's neck and puffed beneath, is altogether easier to place: it is surely an ingenious play on the Médici collar borrowed from Rubens' *Life of Marie de Médici* by the Empress Josephine to raise the cultural tone at the imperial court. Mme Vigée-Lebrun was a great admirer of Rubens' work.

Fichus and *buffons* in fashion plates and paintings at first glance often appear to be made of simple cotton, muslin or lawn. Closer examination, for instance of Mme Vigée-Lebrun's portrait, shows that they were often exquisitely embroidered. This was, perhaps, particularly true from about 1790, when coloured thread was no longer acceptable.[24] As so few examples are now extant, everyone owes a great debt of gratitude to the Los Angeles County Museum of Art for mounting a

19 Buffon, English, late eighteenth century. Square-shaped with white cotton chain- and knotted-stitch embroidery on a white cotton mull ground. When the buffon is folded into a triangle, the floral embroidery on back and front are in perfect alignment.

magnificent exhibition, 'An Elegant Art'. The superb example of a late eighteenth-century English *buffon*, or handkerchief, as it was still often called (the French term 'fichu' being very rarely used), is taken from it. It is decorated with exquisite whitework (fig. 19).

The *fichu menteur* of the early 1790s was particularly interesting in that it hid the neck, very much in the manner of the cravats worn by the *incroyables* (see figs 14, 18 and 20). It was usually made of plain lawn and worn with a coloured shawl which featured appliqué work.

With the Directory period, the shape of the fichu changed completely, because of the change in the silhouette of the dress (see colour plate 3). The Antique influence was reflected in a chemise, which at its simplest was made of sheer muslin gathered under the breasts, giving it an extremely high waist in contrast to the elongated waist of the previous decade. Necklines revealed more of the breasts than they concealed. The fichus and *buffons* which had covered the *décolletage* to achieve the 'pouter-pigeon' effect of the 1780s and early 1790s were now no longer an aid to modesty. They were

21   *Fashion plate from Heideloff's* The Gallery of Fashion, *1794. French ladies also sported the 'snake' stole, although they continued to call it a palatine.*

20   *Fashion plate from the* Journal de la Mode et du Goût, *1 January 1793. The model wears her plain lawn* fichu menteur *with a blue shawl which has three rows of white ribbons. The magazine points out the fashion during the early years of the French Revolution for ribbons appliquéd in striped patterns to shawls.*

cut along the shoulders, crossed directly under the breasts, and tied behind. As if to enhance the exposure of the bosom, the fichu was made in a colour which provided a sharp contrast with the plain muslin dress.

FROM OLD-FASHIONED TIPPET TO NEW-FANGLED SNAKE

Tippets, which had been so fashionable in the seventeenth century, lingered into the eighteenth. In place of the rather cumbersome furs that had been donned in the past, the tippet, in the words of a specialist on eighteenth-century dress, had become a 'small shoulder cape or scarf of various materials, wrapped around the neck and either falling over the bosom, or twisted and tucked into the top of the bodice'.[25] The wearers appear to have striven for a light and wispy look. The *Weekly Register* noted in 1735: 'Laced tippets much worn; some had diamond solitaires [i.e. single gems] to hook them together.' A still lighter alternative was a feather tippet, worn in the first half of the eighteenth century.[26] Towards the end of the century it had in some cases shrunk still further: 'No handkerchief, but a narrow piece of plaited gauze, by way of a tippet', was a description of 1780.[27] It was doubtless one of these creations that Mrs Delany had in mind when she castigated a lady for wearing 'no more of a tippet than serves to make her bosom conspicuous rather than to hide it'.[28] Nevertheless, fur tippets were also worn alongside these delicate confections, although they were nearly always lighter than in the seventeenth century, being made of sable or ermine.[29]

22   Fashion plate from the Journal des Dames et des Modes, *22 August 1798. The* écharpe agrafée *or 'clasped scarf' lent variety to the simple classical line.*

In the late eighteenth century, when the ubiquitous long white chemise and redingote (both worn to imitate classical drapery) had helped to recreate an idyllic past, a serpent suddenly appeared. He can be seen looped around the neck with an air of insouciant innocence in some of the Heideloff fashion plates of 1794. Soon he would be knotted around the neck, or wound around the body in long sinuous curves. Often the ladies of the fashion plates would also clasp to themselves enormous fur muffs, as if to boast that no snake was too big to be denied a fond embrace. The most striking accessories to set off these stoles were the enormous feathers that rear snake-like above the heads of their wearers. This is surely a beautiful and remarkable style, but it would be interesting to know if so much costumary provocation and bravado would have been possible without the Revolution that had begun five years earlier in France.

The 'snake' was really too *outré* to be assimilated into neo-classical fashion. The long simple stole, like the one shown at the beginning of this study, was far commoner and more in keeping with the Antique (see fig. 2). A rare alternative was the *écharpe agrafée*, or clasped scarf. When it appeared in 1798 at the Parisian gardens of Tivoli, a favourite stamping-ground of the fashionable, it was received with rapturous applause by the editor of Europe's leading fashion periodical, the *Journal des Dames et des Modes*. What he commended in particular was the magnificent draped effect which complemented, rather than detracted from, the classical line.[30]

TURQUERIE

The Orient, formerly an object merely of idle curiosity, was given a secure place in the civilization of the eighteenth century. The educated public became more discriminating in its taste for orientalism, and distinguished more carefully between the different areas of the East. For most of the century it was not the Orient in general, but Turkey, and above all India, that seized the popular imagination.

Serious interest in Turkey went back to the very beginning of the century. In 1700 the Duke of Chartres held a masquerade at Marly which figured the Grand Turk and his menagerie. The masquerade was clearly an 'event', and was described at length in the *Mercure*, which reported that the 'costumes were magnificent'.[31] It was the French again, shortly afterwards, who provided Europe, and more especially England, with the first really accurate record of Turkish dress. In 1714 there appeared a collection of one hundred engravings, commissioned by the French Ambassador in Constantinople, and based on the drawings of J.B. Vanmour, who had depicted them from life there. Contemporaries at once

23 Lady Mary Wortley Montagu, engraved by W.
Greatbatch after an original miniature of c. 1720. The
popularity of turquerie owed much to Lady Mary's
inspiration.

appreciated their authenticity, which was further recognized when Vanmour's drawings were paid the compliment of inclusion in Thomas Jefferys' famous masquerade pattern book of 1757. Their presence there ensured that they would have an important influence on England's fashions, which so often took their inspiration from masquerade, while masquerade *en turque* was particularly widespread in England by the mid-century.[32] The theatre, too, added its enormous prestige to aid the diffusion of *turquerie*. When *Les Trois Sultanes* was staged in Paris in 1761, the costumes of the women were actually made up in Constantinople from native materials.[33] Before long *turquerie* was adopted at the French court, thus gaining the seal of respectability. In 1755 Mme de Pompadour commissioned Van Loo to execute a series of portraits representing her as a sultana; Mme du Barry had herself painted in similar fashion eighteen years later.

In England the chief popularizer of *turquerie* was Lady Mary Wortley Montagu. Contemporaries were fascinated by her intimate knowledge of Turkish life, which included a visit to a harem. Her intriguing letters about Turkey were widely circulated before becoming a best-seller when published on her death in 1763. In the engraving of Lady Mary Wortley Montagu by W. Greatbatch she is depicted wearing a turban, the accessory most closely associated with the Turks in the minds of the fashionable. Throughout most of the eighteenth century turbans were to be in vogue for formal dress among women, and also for informal wear for men, usually with their banyans. In many cases turbans were worn with a scarf underneath which hung down behind the head and shoulders, as in fig. 23. As for other Turkish garments, a scarf worn as a sash around the waist, and the kaftan, were widely adopted. The garment most prized by Lady Mary herself was the *curdee*, which she was wearing in 1717 while her husband was British Ambassador to the Porte. She describes it as: 'a loose robe they throw off or put on according to the weather, being of a rich brocade (mine is green and gold), either lined with ermine or sables; the sleeves reach very little below the shoulders.'[34]

It is hard to measure the influence of Lady Mary Wortley Montagu on eighteenth-century dress. Innumerable portraits, often professedly of her, but in reality of others modelling her dress, bear witness to public interest. Yet, as an eccentric by even the standards of the eighteenth century, she was on the fringes of, rather than in the main stream of, fashion; an inspirer of fashions rather than the deviser of any particular one.[35]

Turquerie for men – the turbans so often worn by women apart – seems on the whole to have been more

part of everyday wear. The nightgown, or banyan, as it was sometimes called in the eighteenth century, was highly fashionable for informal wear. Richardson's portrait shows Lord Burlington in the imposing 'undress' of a scarlet nightgown, to underline his claim to be an architect and classed among the artists and intellectuals who loved to affect this blend of the exotic and informal.[36] Hayman's portrait of Maurice Greene, Professor of Music at Cambridge, in a far looser banyan, probably gives a better idea of of how artists and intellectuals below the peerage looked (figs. 24 and 25).

THE SHAWL AS 'THE GIFT OF PRINCES'

When King Ashurnasirpal II (see fig. 1) donned his shawl to officiate as High Priest of the Assyrians, he was fortunately unaware that a later version of the sacred garment would be worn in the distinctive gaudy colours of aniline dyes, to be flaunted by Victorian prostitutes in search of clients. Herodotus, who in the fifth century BC described a woollen covering that was clearly a shawl, being worn by the Egyptians, would perhaps have been less astonished to learn of its diverse uses. Nonetheless, even this broad-minded historian might have been surprised to learn that the garment was to adorn women. The *shal*, as worn in India, was a male garment; its degree of fineness reflected, not the wearer's personal taste, but his social status.[37] Far from being designed as a luxurious wrap for a fashionable lady, the shawl had originally been the traditional gift of an Indian prince to his vassal.[38] The delicacy of these early Indian shawls is very apparent in the illuminated manuscript at the British Museum which shows Abdullah Qutb-Shah of Golconda proudly wearing his *kashmir* shawl about the year 1670 (fig. 26).[39]

It was not surprising, therefore, that the first shawls adopted by Europeans in the sub-continent, and no doubt when on leave in Europe itself, were worn by men. Captain Foote of the British East India Company, as painted by Reynolds about 1761-5, certainly shows a robust sense that the shawl was intended for masculine attire. He wears two: one around his left shoulder as a stole and the other as a sash about his waist (fig. 27).

'I dreamt . . . that thou camest into the room with a shawl in thy hand . . . that you folded the shawl about my waist.'[40] In these words Laurence Sterne seems to chide his friend Eliza for usurping an article of male dress, and to ask for its return to his own sex. If, as seems likely, Eliza brought back some shawls with her to London on her return from Bombay in 1765, she could even have been instrumental in starting the fashion for women wearing shawls which began about this time.[41] Sterne may also have been struck by the novelty of this development, whoever started it. For in the second half of the

Earl of Burlington

It is hard to know when precisely the fashion for Kashmir shawls was established in England. Miss Pamela Clabburn, one of the foremost authorities on the subject, has found no examples among fashionable portraits before the 1780s. She feels that their absence earlier was hardly surprising, as 'shawls with their supple qualities of drapery would not have gone well with the stiff silks which were the hallmarks of fashionable dressing up to the 1780s'.[43] Shawls seem to have entered the wardrobes of fashionable ladies as part of neo-classical dress pioneered in the 1760s. The use of the 'Greek style' first for informal wear would explain the dearth of portraits in which subjects tended to be depicted in the full finery of formal attire.

The earliest example of a portrait sitter in a shawl *à la grecque* seems to be Lady Margaret Bingham, who was painted by Angelica Kauffmann in 1767 (located at Althorp). The artist was one of the first in England to visit the excavations at Herculaneum and Pompeii, and she must rank, alongside Vien with his *La Marchande des Amours*, as one of the initiators of 'the Greek look'. What is particularly interesting for the dress historian is the prominence that Angelica Kauffmann accords the shawl in the portrait: it contributes almost more than anything else to the draped effect which was the fashion's essential quality. When one of Gainsborough's sitters, Viscountess Molyneux, was shown clutching a black shawl to her bosom two years later, the fashion for shawls may be said to have 'arrived' (see fig. 28).

As for the wearing of *kashmirs*, the vogue appears to have started around 1777. In a letter of 17 April in that year, it was reported that: 'The shawls all come from Cassemire . . . [their] material the produce of a Thibet sheep.'[44]

Within about a decade *kashmirs* had become assimilated to one of the most powerful artistic movements of the time – the 'return to the Antique'. It would be foolish to look for a single cause for this swift and complex development. Nonetheless, a charming *bacchante* in Naples may surely claim some of the credit. Lady Emma Hamilton is remembered now primarily as Nelson's mistress. For the fashionable society of the day, however, Lady Hamilton was the modeller of Grecian costume who brought the Antique to life. Her husband, Sir William Hamilton, the British Ambassador in Naples, had educated a whole generation in the classical past by the publication in 1766–7 of four magnificent folio volumes in which some of the finest engravers of the day recorded his remarkable collection of antiquities. And then, after the scholarly introduction to the world of Pompeii, the intimate performances at the British Embassy: before a mesmerized audience Lady Hamilton staged the

24-5 *Lord Burlington, by J. Richardson, c. 1717–20, and Maurice Greene, by Francis Hayman, 1747 (detail). Two contrasting styles of banyan favoured by artists and intellecturals: Lord Burlington enchances the aura of* turquerie *with his silk turban and sash, while the professor of music, Maurice Greene, is more informally dressed in his fine red damask gown.*

seventeenth century, when 'ships trading with the East brought back oblongs of fine woollen fabrics with unfamiliar colourful designs . . . then known as *schal, scial* or *chal* [they] do not immediately appear to have been worn in Europe but were probably kept to be admired or used as light rugs'.[42] The word *shal* at that time, therefore, referred not to a garment, but the material – a meaning which lingered for a long time to come. Even in the nineteenth century no shawl was considered worthy of the name, if it were not made of material woven in Kashmir, or at the very least purported to imitate it.

26 *Abdullah Qutb-Shah of Golconda, miniature from the Golconda School of Painting, c. 1670. Typical of the* kashmirs *of the period was the shawl's border of semi-naturalistic plants.*

27 *Captain Foote, by Sir Joshua Reynolds, c. 1761–5. This sitter (whose costume depicted here survives to this day), like other members of the British East India Company, returned home with many shawls from Kashmir.*

◁ *28 Viscountess Molyneux, by Thomas Gainsborough, 1769. Her black silk shawl, edged with lace and worn with a striped light silk polonaise, provides a good example of the more informal wear becoming fashionable in late eighteenth-century England.*

the greatest artists have rejoiced to be able to produce. Standing, kneeling, sitting, lying down, grave or sad, playful, exulting, repentant, wanton, menacing, anxious – all mental states follow rapidly one after another. With wonderful taste she suits the folding of her veil to each expression, and with the same handkerchief makes every kind of headdress.[45]

Goethe described Lady Hamilton's 'attitudes' in his capacity as one of Europe's most brilliant writers. Her influence also sank deep into the world of fashion itself. In her *Memoirs* the comtesse de Boigne tells how she and her aristocratic friends played supporting roles to Lady Hamilton in 1792. It was, however, the star's performance with two or three *kashmirs* that commanded attention.[46]

If Lady Hamilton had remained in Italy throughout the period, her influence on fashion might have been confined to those who made the Grand Tour. In May 1791 she returned to England where she enchanted devotees of the Antique 'by wearing and popularizing in London, the original classical style in which Sir William had dressed her on her first arrival in Naples'.[47] George Romney, one of Reynolds' principal rivals, was so bewitched by her that he persuaded her to sit for him again and again. Thomas Baxter and other British artists also dressed their sitters after Lady Hamilton's 'attitudes'. Even in France Lady Hamilton seems to have been paid the compliment of imitation, as one of the great leaders of fashion at the turn of the century, Mme Récamier, also entertained her guests with a shawl dance.

'attitudes' in which she delighted to recreate the *bacchantes* in the frescoes of the villa of Cicero. These extraordinary modelling displays are probably best seen through the eyes of Goethe, who was one of the many entranced by them. He recorded in *Travels in Italy*, under 16 March 1787:

The old knight had made for her a Greek costume, which becomes her perfectly. Dressed in this, and letting her hair loose, and taking a couple of shawls, she exhibits every possible variety of posture, expression and look, so that at the last the spectator almost fancies it a dream. One beholds here in perfection, in movement, in ravishing variety, all that

As France was to be the principal European home of the *kashmir* for much of the period, it is worth following its early history there in some detail. It is related in the charming contemporary *History of a Shawl* by de Jouy, the self-styled Hermit of the Chaussée d'Antin, that when the duc d'Aiguillon gave one to Mme du Barry, the former mistress of Louis XV, 'even the name of this oriental material was unknown'. Although the ladies of the court examined it with great interest, they decided unanimously that it was totally lacking in grace, a verdict that amounted to a sentence of banishment for the rest of the ancien régime.[48] That has not prevented the French, however, from claiming credit for adopting the cone motif in the cotton works of Oberkampf at Jouy as early as

29 Lady Emma Hamilton as a *bacchante, engraved by
Thomas Piroli, 1794. Her shawl dances were widely
imitated, especially in France.*

◁ *30 Fashion plate from the* Journal de la Mode et du Goût, *5 June 1790. This is the earliest example of an illustration of a shawl from Kashmir in a French fashion periodical, where it is described significantly as* toilette anglaise. *The superb grace with which the shawl is worn here was soon to be cultivated in academies opened specially for that purpose.*

de Thélusson the same year provides an interesting comparison with the fashion plate. The sitter was in the forefront of the fashionable 'return to the Antique'. France's outstanding architect in the style, Ledoux, had built her a town house in Paris which was very widely admired and indeed, ravishingly beautiful. The dress of the marquise in the portrait probably gives a better idea of what France's social élite were wearing than the periodical, which prescribed fashion for those just below them in the social scale. The marquise is robed *à l'antique*, in the simple draped style that connoisseurs alone found authentic. That the dress is close to those worn by contemporaries is clear from a description in the *Souvenirs* of Elisabeth Vigée-Lebrun, where she recalls having seen Queen Marie-Antoinette and her circle in similar white muslin gowns as early as *c.* 1775.[52] The fact that this portrait is by David himself provides a strong case for accepting its costumary accuracy. David was profoundly convinced of the important part of dress in the 'return to the Antique', and in his portraits he helped both to pioneer and to reflect the latest fashions. He was, in effect, insufficiently imaginative to innovate in fashion, but endowed with the sensitivity to bring out fashion's inner development. Particularly noticeable in this portrait is the artful informality with which the shawl is worn. The accessory itself is more stole-like than the shawls reproduced in the *Journal de la Mode et du Goût*. Yet, it has more the appearance of genuine *kashmir*. The small area of the design enhances the neo-classical effect, as it sets off the draped statuesque appearance of the sitter just enough to bring her to life, without jeopardizing the aura of the Antique. As for the pattern on the border of the shawl, it closely resembles a fragment in the Victoria & Albert Museum of a *kashmir* of the eighteenth century (fig. 32). Paisley, in the nineteenth century, was often to reproduce what was called the 'spade' design in its attempt to imitate *kashmirs*.

1766.[49] As far as the shawl itself was concerned, they not only rejected it in 1775; as late as 1788, when 'genuine *kashmirs* were being sent from India as presents to French women', they were 'cut up for petticoats instead of being used as intended'.[50] When Kashmir shawls did come into vogue in France, in 1790, they were described as 'an English fashion'.

A full shawl was featured on 5 June 1790, in the *Journal de la Mode et du Goût*:

> For a long time English fashions have formed part of those of France. Their distinctive mark is a simple but compact effect, which our French ladies are sometimes pleased to imitate. The shawls, a type of unusually ample handkerchief, hail from India, where they replace mantles. Adopted by the English, they have come to France and go rather well with fashionable undress. The English woman shown in this plate wears one of these shawls. The background is white, the surrounding border is composed of green leaves with red and blue flowers, and the fringe is made up of the colours of the nation [red, white and blue].[51]

Jacques-Louis David's portrait of the marquise de Sorcy

31 Marquise de Sorcy de Thélusson, by Jacques-Louis ▷ *David, 1790. This is one of the first portraits in France to show the long rectangular* kashmir. *It is of écru, or unbleached colour, with the fashionable 'spade' design.*

32 *Fragment of a kashmir, eighteenth century. The
'spade' design was very distinctive of real kashmirs and
was often imitated at Paisley.*

To study the shapes and materials of shawls in the late
eighteenth century, no better source can be used than
the *Journal des Dames et des Modes*. The periodical was
founded by an ex-Oratorian priest, Pierre de La
Mésangère, who had all the clergy's obsessive interest
in fashion, together with the gifts of a journalistic genius.

33 *Fashion plate from the* Journal des Dames et des Modes, *25 November 1797. The shawl was often transformed in France into a long stole, called a* schall uni.

emphasize the sweep of the drapery. A typical example can be found in the 25 November 1797 number of the *Journal*. It would be hard to better the editor's lucid commentary there on the *schall uni*:

> These are the most common. And if they are not the richest, they are incontestably the most elegant. In addition, it is one of the most ancient fashions that we have. Formerly, shawls were square and were worn in the manner of a fichu. For about a year they have been long and narrow. Rose, violet, canary are the favourite colours. The shawl ordinarily covers the shoulders, but sometimes they are worn crosswise.[53]

34 *Fashion plate from the* Journal des Dames et des Modes, *July 1797. The model wears a rose-coloured* schall uni *of transparent lawn and bearing the Grecian ring motif, which complements perfectly the white neo-classical chemise.*

He provides an unrivalled inventory of fashions from June 1797 to the *Journal*'s demise some forty years later. As La Mésangère shows, all types of material were used, and only at the very end of the century were genuine *kashmirs* found in any abundance. The chief cause of this hiatus in the adoption of shawls from Kashmir must surely have been the Revolutionary Wars which inevitably inhibited trade with India, while the flourishing smuggling trade with England may not have got properly under way until the time of Napoleon.

One of the French Directory's signal achievements in the field of fashion was to transform the shawl into a kind of stole, called the *schall uni*, which admirably set off the statuesque neo-classical line. The *schall uni* was very long, and usually of a single plain colour in the same material as the dress. The accessory's plain colours went admirably with the white chemise, and helped

The *schall uni* was to be seen everywhere, in Boilly's *La Marche Incroyable*, Chataignier's 'Audience of the Directory', in Desrais's *Promenade du Boulevard des Italiens* and elsewhere. An attractive variation to solid single colours was the use of transparent material. A typical example appeared in the *Journal des Dames et des Modes* in July 1797. The shawl here is interesting for its use of the Grecian ring design, which had appeared earlier on the borders of the long shawl worn by Mme Tallien in David's magnificent portrait of 1794–5. The transparent *schall uni* of the late 1790s was particularly effective in adding a further and subtler emphasis to the draped effect of the gown beneath.

However popular the *schall uni*, the significance of the revived interest in *kashmirs* did not escape contemporaries. In the number of the *Journal des Dames et des Modes* for 18 November 1798, the editor wrote of the effect of public events on fashion, and singled out the Egyptian Campaign.[54] A month later there appeared an illustration of one of the *kashmirs* mentioned there. Yet it is interesting that Bonaparte's wife Josephine, who as Empress was later to turn the taste for shawls into a real passion, was quite unimpressed by those which her husband had sent her from Eqypt in 1798. She wrote to her son, Eugène de Beauharnais, who had himself accompanied the expedition to Egypt, 'I find them hideous. Their great advantage lies in their lightness, but I doubt very much if they will ever become fashionable.'[55]

---

35 *Mme Tallien, by Jacques-Louis David, c. 1794–5. She epitomizes the Antique style of the Directoire* élégantes. *Her simple white chemise, tied at the shoulder, is also secured at the waist by a blue sash. Her yellow woollen shawl is bordered with the much-favoured black Grecian ring design.*

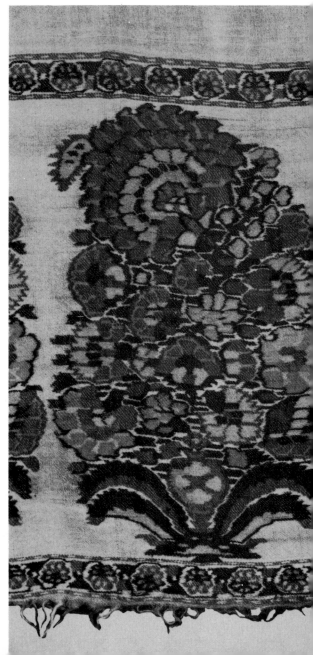

As if to mock the future Empress, *kashmirs* at once became the rage. It was as if the years of neglect had created an insatiable appetite for them. Even La Mésangère, the astute observer of feminine fashions, had never seen anything like it. Looking back in 1815, a year that marked the final fall of Napoleon's Empire but left feminine fashions largely untouched, he recalled the stirring times when *kashmirs* were introduced into France:

Our beauties invented a thousand reasons why that taste 'for *kashmirs*' should be satisfied. The richest had only to pronounce those words, so omnipotent in their mouths: it is the fashion; women of the second rank insisted on the necessity of doing like everyone else; those further down the scale pleaded reasons of health and economy: a *kashmir*, said they, lasts for a very long time and dispenses with the need for a complete outfit. Finally, people who had no plausible reason for the purchase relied on that refrain, so powerful with the weak or amorous: if you don't give me a *kashmir* dress, it is because you don't love me.[56]

---

36 *Border of a* kashmir, *c. 1750–1800. The motif shown here, known as the* buta *(literally 'flower') in the West was called the cone or pine. The geometric, angular outline of each petal was a prominent feature of the twill-tapestry technique.*

THE SHAWL AS MANUFACTURED PRODUCT

A *kashmir* manufactured in Europe: it is as well to recognize at the outset that this ambition could never be realized. The cultural differences of two continents opposed it, and so also did a mountain goat. If cultural barriers might sometimes be crossed, the goat had an obstinacy that could seldom be overcome.

All authorities are agreed that among the shawl's irresistible allurements were the unrivalled suppleness and soft texture of the wool, which were the mountain goat's response to the challenge of the freezing Himalayas. In a period when fashionable ladies often shivered in their thin classical chemises, Kashmir shawls were sometimes prized as much for their warmth as for their exotic appearance.

The inescapable fact that the Tibetan goat was indigenous to the Himalayas was one reason why the Europeans were never able to manufacture a convincing imitation of the shawl from Kashmir. As early as 1774, Warren Hastings, the powerful British Governor-General of India, had appreciated the vital importance of obtaining the right wool, and had tried without success to establish *Capra hircus* in Britain. After a second attempt by Hastings had failed a decade later, another abortive effort was made by the imposingly styled Society for the Improvement of British Wool.[57] British and French manufacturers, who despaired of obtaining the goat's fleece itself, tried to imitate its unique texture by using 'Botany worsted' (Australian wool), Spanish flockwool, and various combinations especially of wool and silk, notably 'Persian yarn', in which silk and merino wool were combined.[58] Yet, however diligently the manufacturers sought a substitute, *Capra hircus* had, so to speak, the last bleat.

The second inimitable feature of the best-known *kashmirs* was the traditional working method of the Indian craftsmen. In Miss Clabburn's measured words, 'the Indian weaver wove his shawls very slowly indeed, using a technique which took no account of time'.[59] These immemorial techniques were rather akin to those used in European tapestry weaving, and involved using a separate shuttle for each colour. For the untechnically minded, the process is probably best described as similar to the making of mosaics, composed of many patterned pieces, embroidered separately and sewn together (see fig. 36).[60] Without employing those methods, the resulting artefact was utterly different. The contrast between the two is highlighted so well by Sarah Pauly in her introduction to the delightful exhibition, 'The Kashmir Shawl' at Yale University Art Gallery, that it seems worth quoting here *in extenso*:

European shawls, whether woven on the drawloom

or the Jacquard loom, were always machine-woven, while the Indian product was always made by hand-manipulated weaving (when not embroidered). This difference is crucial, though subtle and somewhat difficult to make out. As Levitt says of European shaws, '. . . construction of cloth became limited to what a machine could do'. Those limitations are both technical and aesthetic. Though the Jacquard loom overcame the drawloom's limited design range, neither could be used to create the mosaic-like patterning of double-interlocking twill-tapestry, which can be created only by hand . . . The rhythms of a machine are essentially different from those of the human hand, and shawls are a reflection of those rhythms.[61]

Probably the greatest failing of the machine was its regularity and the over-precise definition of the pattern, endlessly and wearisomely repeated. It was, in short, a classic case of a contrast between the thinking craftsman and the unthinking machine, and in an area where the difference was particularly hard to disguise.

A third divergence which sprang from both the materials used and the methods of production was the 'back to back' arrangement of the Indian shawl. To overcome the roughness of the underside, real Kashmir shawls were usually woven in pairs and sewn together. An important exception was the famous 'ring shawl', so called because it was so finely woven that it could be drawn through a ring. That was possible only because these shawls were single colour, without the super-imposed design that added to the bulk of the better-known Kashmir shawl.

Finally, there was the problem of the cultural gap between the Indian craftsman and the European factory hand. The art style of shawls from Kashmir was a blend of Hindu and Arab ideas. The pine or cone, the motif beloved above all others by the Indian craftsman, held a deep religious significance. It had originated in Chaldea, where it was known simply as the Tree of Life. It is basically a floral pattern with the flowers, leaves and stems conventionalized and represented in an arbitrary outer shape. That itself was a new development that crystallized around the middle of the eighteenth century.[62] The move from a far freer design with far greater individual variations may itself have seemed to some a derogation from the Hindu ideal of individual enlightenment. The hardening of the design still further through the 'perfection' of factory methods can only have seemed to the Indian craftsmen outright desecration.

It was hubris for Europeans to try to manufacture *kashmirs*. Yet, like Prometheus, they brought benefits as well as harm. In this case, they tried to 'scale heaven' in at least three places: Norwich, Edinburgh and the west of Scotland, while the story of their French counterparts, notably Lyons, Paris and Jouy (despite the latter's claim to have adopted the pine motif in 1766) either began at the very end of the eighteenth century, or belongs entirely to the nineteenth.

Norwich, by virtue of Edward Barrow's manufactory which began in 1784, is given credit by common consent for producing the first British shawls. Their origins appear to have been very modest. 'These were not shawls in the true sense of the word', insists one of the leading authorities, 'but a kind of cotton neckerchief of small dimensions embroidered in imitation of the flowered muslin neckerchiefs of Bengal. Moreover, they were cheap products intended for export primarily to America.' More important in many ways was the contribution of John Harvey, who experimented throughout the 1780s with Spanish and Norfolk yarns.[63] It was this long-

37 Shawl counterpane, woven with wool on a silk warp, Norwich, 1795. As it was not considered possible at that date to weave in the design, it was embroidered on by hand, using a close darning stitch.

standing experience with the fabric itself that seems to have put Norwich ahead of other aspirant manufacturers of shawls at the end of the eighteenth century. Another important factor was the presence of experienced craftsmen, and, it could be added, the absence of the high-powered machinery that was later to prove so destructive of the shawl's aesthetic appearance. At any rate, Norwich's early success was marked by the award of a silver medal in 1791 by the Royal Society of Arts for a shawl counterpane, woven for the Duke of Norfolk. It was judged 'equal in beauty and far superior in strength to the Indian counterpanes'. Contemporaries were particularly impressed by its size, no less than four yards square, and woven in one piece.[64] In the same year a retailer in Norwich dared to announce that he had on sale 'Norwich and other shawls equal in beauty and wear to those imported from the East Indies'.[65] That was a bold claim, but is supported to some extent by the quality of some of the few specimens that have survived. 'The Norwich shawls', it has been said, 'have a striking clarity of design, which distinguishes them and clearly relates them to the early Cashmeres.'[66] That commendation

illustrated in the *Lady's Monthly Museum* of January 1799.[69]

It is sad that no examples of eighteenth-century shawls from Edinburgh seem to be extant. 'The finest and most costly of all early imitation shawls came from Edinburgh', according to the leading authority on the subject. He adds that their brocading technique was not far removed from the tapestry technique of the *kashmir*, to be replaced around 1803 by the harness loom, which severely curtailed aesthetic possibilities.[70]

Although Paisley's story belongs essentially to the nineteenth century, an early centre of shawl printing, as distinct from weaving, existed at Leven Printfield in the west of Scotland. These printed shawls, forerunners of the nineteenth century, are mentioned as early as 1785 in the *Glasgow Mercury*.[71] That early date, together with the evidence of efforts to adapt the design for different sectors of the market, as in 'stout country pattern' and another labelled 'genteel and pretty', seem to show that commercialization of the shawl began in earnest even before the start of the nineteenth century.[72] The example from a print block of *c.* 1794 given here shows on the extreme right the border, to its left the central medallion which would also be used at the four corners of the field. The filling motif or sprig would be on a separate block.[73] It is interesting to see the prominence of the cone motif from Kashmir over-stylized, but still recognizable – words which are perhaps true of much that the Western manufacturers produced in imitation of *kashmirs*.

The shawl had started in India as a 'gift of princes', its fineness an index of social status. It served the same function in Europe as long as its use remained confined to an élite restricted in size by the sheer cost of these magnificent garments. It was an aristocratic garment that did not survive democratic diffusion among the masses in the second half of the nineteenth century. Till then, social snobbery would preserve very passable European imitations. Its true acolytes, like the Empress Josephine, were content, even when war raged throughout Europe, with nothing less than the genuine Indian article.

seems particularly applicable to the shawl counterpane of 1795. The close darning stitches at a short distance rather resemble the weaving in *kashmirs*.[67] Norwich also had the distinction of developing a prized fashion of the period, the shawl dresses which were manufactured by Mr P.J. Knight and worn by Queen Charlotte and her daughters in 1792.[68] A magnificent example of an English shawl dress, made from printed cream silk and woollen shawl lengths, is in the Victoria & Albert Museum (see colour plate 1). The role of the Norwich shawl in completing a fashionable ensemble is described and

3
Shawls: from Craft to Mass Production
1800–1900

The nineteenth century was the Age of the Shawl, as the late eighteenth had been that of the scarf and neo-classical chemise. It was hardly surprising, therefore, that the development of the century's most distinctive accessory charted the course of the great Industrial Revolution. Nowhere is that seen more clearly than in the contrast between the French and British shawls of the period: in France the prolongation of the eighteenth-century tradition of craftsmanship paradoxically seconded by the 'sensitive' Jacquard loom; in Britain the effacement of the 'pre-industrial' centres at Norwich and Edinburgh by the textile factories of Paisley.

THE FRENCH EMPHASIS ON DESIGN

The shawl, which was regarded in Paisley as a manufacturer's product, always retained in France its status as a work of art. So, while the British tended to think in terms of improving production, the French concentrated their attention primarily on artistic design. It was hardly surprising that French imitations were as expensive as they were beautiful. The novels of Balzac, indeed, show that the same could be said of the tiny élite who wore them. Ownership of a *kashmir* in the early nineteenth century was the dream of every young lady and the outward sign of social standing. The important place of the Kashmir shawl in French society is amusingly illustrated in a little 'improving' story related in the *Journal des Dames et des Modes* of 1833. A gallant young man had plunged into the Seine to save a lady from drowning. Hardly had he deposited her on the bank before he jumped in again to salvage her *kashmir*, which he had seen floating in the middle of the river.[1] The message is clear: it was hardly conceivable that any respectable society lady would wish to survive the loss of her Kashmir shawl.

It may be doubted whether the Empress Josephine, who emerged from the dissolute society of the Directory to become Napoleon's mistress and later his wife, would have counted as a 'respectable lady' by the standards of more exacting times. Nonetheless, she was admirably fitted in taste and character to be a worthy successor to Louis XV's Pompadour as a patron of the arts, and even to

surpass her in the world of fashion. Equally important, France, unlike Britain, offered enormous scope to someone with her position and talents.

It is, perhaps, surprising that Josephine was far from enthusiastic about the influx of shawls during Napoleon's Egyptian Campaign. Nonetheless, once converted, and with her husband's purchasing power behind her, she bought and used shawls with an abandon that was the envy of the ladies around her. Mme de Rémusat related in her memoirs how shawls, along with gowns and bonnets, were borne to the Empress in great baskets at her toilette, and that

> she had between 300 and 400 shawls; she used them for dresses, for bed covers and for cushions for her dog to lie on. She always wore one in the morning which she draped over her shoulders more grace-fully than anyone else I have ever seen. Bonaparte, who thought she was too much covered by these shawls, would pull them off and sometimes throw them into the fire. Josephine then called for another.
>
> She bought every shawl that was offered her, whatever the price. She had some that were worth eight, ten and twelve thousand francs. But, indeed, these shawls were one of the great luxuries of this Court. The ladies scorned to appear in a shawl that had cost only fifty louis [1000 francs] and boasted of the price of those they wore.[2]

Even if the Imperial Court were a magnet for the *nouveaux riches*, there is no denying the tasteful attire of the Empress herself. In her portrait by Baron Gros she was depicted in 1809, the year she was divorced by Napoleon, wearing two magnificent shawls. The first, made up into a dress, exhibits the distinctive cone motif to perfection. The second shawl, which is long and red, can be seen draped over Josephine's left shoulder to fall in the form of a train behind her. It could perhaps be claimed that there is a third shawl, a long gauzy veil, adorned delicately with gold edging and tassels. In this instance it is surely equally true that the Empress makes the shawls, and the shawls make the Empress.

1 Shawl dress, English, 1790s. The dress is made from a printed silk and wool shawl, bearing a flower design in pink and green with a *chiné*-like border. The shawl, cut in half and seamed up the centre of the back, has been pleated and stitched on to a lining to follow the shape of the body. The shawl itself, with its borders within the central seam, has remained intact, although the front borders have been faced with green silk. The collar and sleeves of the dress are also of green silk edged with white.

2 'Self-Portrait' by Mme Vigée-Lebrun, 1790. The sharp contrast in dress between black, red and white was sometimes considered by contemporaries to be a sign of intransigent opposition to the French Revolution, an interpretation that would fit the artist's well-known royalist sympathies. Her plain muslin headscarf has been made up into a turban, a favourite fashion accessory. The frilly muslin fichu around her neck is decorated with exquisite embroidery.

3 Fashion plate from the *Journal des Dames et des Modes*, 16 October 1797. The orange fichu and other trimmings serve to enliven the simple classical chemise. While the fichu before the Revolution had been designed, at least ostensibly, as an aid to modesty, here it highlights the *décolletage*, and through being fastened around the high Directory waist, helps to make the breasts still more prominent.

Costume Parisien.   1797.

(8)

Capote Anglaise, garnie en Crêpe, Bandeau de Velours.
Guilloché en Or. Petit fichu croisé. Rubans en Cothurnes.

4 Silk shawl, Spitalfields, *c.* 1810–20. The border, with its roses, acorns, wheat ears and other typical British flowers and plants, which subtly delineate the Kashmir cone motif, shows here at least a perfect match of East and West.

39 *The Empress Josephine, by Baron Gros, 1809. Her*
kashmir *shawl-dress has a border design of very stylized*
cones with bending tips.

◁ *40   Mme Rivière, by Ingres, c. 1805. The artist has caught the beauty of the kashmir (and of the sitter) down to the last delicate tint, notably the warm off-white background of the unbleached shawl and the subtle turquoise, ochre and coral of the finely delineated cone motif.*

Josephine seems to exemplify in her portrait the competing claims of neo-classicists and Romantics. As the Empress gazes pensively at an antique bust, against a background of classical ruins, she leans towards a vase of flowers of uncompromising modernity, while resting her hand on a fine leather-bound book which seems to comprise those illuminated manuscripts which she, and

---

41   Portrait of a Woman, by Henry-François Mulard, c. 1810. A silk Scottish plaid scarf is knotted casually to frame the sitter's fine Médici collar, and is held in place by a striped silk sash around her high Empire waist. The romantic feeling of the portrait is enhanced by the circuitous lines of the shawl, which would appear to be French rather than Indian, to judge by the absence of the cone motif, and the naturalistic rendering of the flowers, while the short regular fringe has a rather machine-made look.

the troubadour painters she patronized, so much admired. Nowhere is her personal preference for Romanticism more clearly demonstrated than in her own clothes. The shawls, veil and tasselled cords offset the severity of the classical chemise almost to the point of submerging it altogether, as the Empress stands in her carefully contrived 'negligence'.

If there were any doubt that the shawl was the outstanding fashion accessory of the Romantics, a moment's glance at the portrait of Mme Rivière by Ingres should be enough to dispel it. The sitter wears a shawl of natural unbleached colour (écru) with a very beautiful cone design, similar to the eighteenth-century example at the Victoria & Albert Museum, already discussed (see fig. 36). The mosaic patterning of the original is brilliantly evoked by Ingres, the painter recommended specifically for his depiction of *kashmirs* by the leading British authority on the subject.[3] The artist was, indeed, well suited by his family background for rendering these textures. His grandfather had been a master tailor, while his wife, described as 'the only person with the slightest influence on her husband', had been a *modiste*.[4] Ingres, as a painter, always appreciated the peculiarly 'three-dimensional' character of the Kashmir shawl:

> Design formerly had been conceived on the flat, even when intended for costume. But Kashmir shawls were seen at their best when hanging in folds, with their curved motifs offset by the human body. Although European designers had been slow to grasp this idea, once assimilated it came to influence a very large field.[5]

In the warmth of its colour, in the luxurious curve of its line and in its sensual texture, the *kashmir* fascinated, even seduced, the Romantics.

For the French and even the English, Scotland was as mysterious and Romantic as India itself. Scottish influences in France dated back long before their supposed inception in 1814 with the arrival in Paris of Highlanders as part of the British army of occupation. As early as the summer of 1806, the *Journal des Dames et des Modes* carried two plates showing ladies wearing Scottish scarves.[6] It is, however, the magnificent *Portrait of a Woman* of about 1810 by Mulard, one of David's students, that best brings out the full extent of these Scottish influences. Together with the plaid scarf, knotted with almost Byronic abandon, the sitter wears a French shawl loosely draped around her arms. Other 'Romantic' features are the abbreviated Médici collar and lace sleeves. As seen in Horace Vernet's fashion plate of 1811 in *Le Bon Genre*, eclecticism could sometimes be carried to absurd lengths: sixteenth-century puffs on the sleeves and ruff at the neck, accompanied by the inevitable Kashmir shawl – the principal vestimentary symbol of Romanticism.

Design itself did not become an issue with the French manufacturers until well into the Empire. At first they were content to imitate the designs of Kashmir itself. It was for their closeness to the originals that the *Journal des Dames et des Modes* in 1803 commended the designs of France's leading manufacturers, the Ternaux brothers.[7] The manufacture of Kashmir shawls in France was further stimulated in 1806 when Napoleon imposed his Berlin Decrees, in which he prohibited imports form overseas.

By 1810 the manufacture of French Kashmir shawls was thriving to the point that there was criticism in the country's leading fashion periodical, the *Journal des Dames et des Modes*, of 'the over-skilful copyists' who showed so little inventive power of their own.[8] As if taking their cue from the *Journal*, the Ternaux brothers the following year petitioned the Minister of the Interior for official backing in producing shawls 'more in conformity with French taste'.

> We wish that His Majesty would acquire twelve only to give as presents to ladies of the Court. We do not doubt that by this means they would be keenly sought after, that the mode would take hold of Paris all the more easily, and from there the whole of Europe, that taste frequently changes where this type of article is concerned, and that people are beginning to get tired of the Indian *palmes* [i.e. cones] without tiring of the article itself . . . Your Excellency will make even more certain of the success of our plans if he approaches one of His Majesty's painters, Isabey, whose style is well known, asking him to negotiate with us over the choice of designs.[9]

The Minister's prompt and positive response shows the enormous advantage to French manufacturers in being able to call on the resources of a centralized state to forward their work. Twelve shawls were ordered immediately at a cost of 24,000 livres, with Isabey commissioned to design them, and when completed were given to the new Empress, Marie-Louise, and her ladies-in-waiting, who carried them around ostentatiously, with the desired result of starting the fashion in Paris. A few weeks later the government's newspaper, the *Moniteur Universel*, announced unctuously:

> The shawls of MM. Ternaux are a perfect product. The designs are the work of our best artists and they are different from the bizarre and confused designs

that one finds on the foreign [i.e. Kashmir] shawls. The *palmes* [i.e. cones] are replaced by bouquets and garlands imitating the most beautiful European flowers, of which the clear colours and fine nuances have something of the appearance of painting . . .[10]

To judge from some of Ternaux's designs that survive, for once the imperial government was telling the truth. The shawls of the Ternaux brothers were very different from those of Kashmir. In place of the natural colour of the goat's fleece for a background was dazzling white, and for the concentrated mosaic-style flowers was substituted a spacious display of naturalistic blooms and tendrils. The effect, in short, was very French and modern, rather reminiscent of the light-hearted neo-classical designs of Percier and Fontaine. The resulting shawls were certainly far from equalling the originals in beauty. At the same time, the abandonment of an inappropriate primitive model helped the French designers to achieve more of their own artistic potential.[11]

The early history of shawl manufacture in France is practically synonymous with that of the Ternaux Company, as was shown by the contemporary practice of referring to all French shawls as Ternaux shawls.[12] And, indeed, it was Guillaume Ternaux who imported some of the shawl goats in 1818 and manufactured the 'Thibet' shawl at Lyons from a yarn made from a combination of silk and wool. It was also the Ternaux brothers who, by using the drawloom and afterwards the Jacquard loom, made it possible for the French in Nîmes and Lyons, as well as Paris, to come close to reproducing the texture of the Indian shawls – and by 1834, at a quarter of the cost. It was above all in the quality of the designs, however, that the French excelled. It was calculated in 1835 that French shawl manufacturers were spending 10% of their gross capital on designing alone. And even a British report of 1839 acknowledged: 'Lyons beat us and indeed the rest of the world, chiefly by the superiority of her patterns, and the excellence of taste displayed in designs.' Wholesale pirating of threads, techniques and designs by British manufacturers testified to the superiority of the Ternaux shawls. The latter even supplanted Indian shawls as models for the British copyists.[13]

---

42   Fashion plate by Horace Vernet in Le Bon Genre, ▷ *1811. The artist, always the witty caricaturist of the latest fashions, shows how a 'profusion of trimmings' has reduced a fine Kashmir shawl to just one of many romantic traits.*

43 'Nou-Rouz' shawl, 389 × 165 cm, French, 1839. It was designed by Amédée Couder and woven by the Paris firm of Gaussen Aîné et Cie. The theme may have been inspired by a shawl described in a French fashion journal of 1839, and presented to Queen Victoria by the Shah of Persia.

In the 1830s and 1840s the French had one of the most inventive, and surely also one of the most perverse, shawl designers of all time. Jean-Baptiste Amédée Couder, son of a designer and the brother of the painter Auguste Couder, has been justly hailed as 'a pioneer before 1848 in the completely new sector of art applied to industry'.[14] Even if that is a bold claim to make in the country of Colbert's famous *manufactures royales*, of Gobelins tapestry and Sèvres porcelain, few would deny that he revolutionized the designs of Kashmir shawls both in France and India. Starting from the conviction that Indian shawl patterns distorted Persian designs, he banished the ubiquitous cone, and replaced it by the most rarified architectural elements and inscriptions. And as if these aesthetic fantasies were insufficient to rivet the attention of contemporaries, he and other French designers actually reorganized native designs in the Punjab. Indian peasants were instructed to execute patterns that Europeans considered more in keeping with oriental taste than their own immemorial designs! Short of instructing the natives on how to drink tea or smoke hashish, it would be hard to conceive how cultural imperialism could have been pushed further. A by-product of this bizarre intervention was that it made it almost impossible thereafter to determine the origin of elements in the designs of *kashmirs*. Whenever a scholar stands with furrowed brows before a shawl, at a loss to know whether it is Indian, or a British or French copy of Indian, or, perhaps, a British copy of an Indian shawl inspired by French orientalism, the celebrated name of Couder risks being coupled with an expletive.

'The Festival of Nou-Rouz', the Persian New Year, is probably Couder's most staggering, and certainly his most famous, design. It created a sensation when it was shown at the Paris Exhibition of 1839. The shawl shows at each end an oriental building in the middle of which the enthroned Shah of Persia receives homage from the high dignitaries of his empire. Around the white centre, strewn with flowers and branches, there is a procession in profile of personages, elephants, horses and camels. As a final touch of spurious authenticity, an Arabic inscription runs along the narrow black borders. Such details, however, are apt to be lost, like the enthroned Shah himself, in this extraordinary architectural pageant, which has something of the force of a surrealist dreamscape.

The Persian New Year betrayed both the hubris of the designer and the versatility of the Jacquard loom. To be more Persian than the Persians was clever, but in doubtful taste. Similarly, the shawl's production, on a Jacquard loom with the use of some 101,000 programming cards to order the design, did more to enhance the manufacturer's reputation than feminine elegance.

If Couder thought that he could dictate taste to the lady of fashion, he was just one of many deluded males. The cone design remained a favourite for decades to come. In fig. 44 it is shown in all its delicate, elaborate sinuosity in an advertisement by a leading French company. As the caption, 'Three in One', cleverly indicates, the look of a shawl depended very much on how it was worn. In a society where elegance was a fine art, such matters of dress were not left to chance. The serious-minded young lady went (or was sent) to classes to be taught how to

△ 44 Advertisement for the 'Perfect Patent Shawl or Three Shawls in One', 1847. The shawl depicted here had become a real outdoor accessory. French manufacturers, abetted by the Jacquard loom, had taken considerable liberties with the Indian cone motif, of which the elongated sinuous tracery covers about half of the whole surface of the shawl.

45   Kashmir, *66 × 72 in., c. 1870. Adaptation for the*
French market is evident in the rendering of the cones,
which are elongated to the point of resembling scrolls
in a medieval manuscript and also in the way that the
'all-over' pattern invades the whole surface, apart from
a small area in the centre.

wear, or more precisely, drape, a shawl, just as she had in the eighteenth century.[15] At the very least she received improving advice from the women's press, as in the article, 'How to wear a shawl', in *Sylvia's Home Journal* of 1861:

> We may add that all shawls should be as much as possible draped upon the woman who wears them, and sustained by the arms being pressed upon the bust; but we must also add that we have only displayed to our readers the material part of this difficult art . . . [there followed what may be termed 'the spiritual dimension' of shawl-wearing].[16]

However skilful the imitations, true devotees were not content with anything other than the genuine article from Kashmir itself. The fine example in fig. 45 dates from about 1870. It took its name of 'harlequin work' from the little cone panels along the right edge, which were woven separately and later stitched on. A feature typical of many other *kashmirs* as well was the way in which the intricate design covered almost the entire surface, apart from the small black central medallion. Again, the dark subdued colours were very common: in this case black, red, pink, violet, ochre and blue.

BRITISH SHAWLS

The manufacture of British shawls can be best understood in the context of the Industrial Revolution. The early centres, notably Edinburgh and Norwich, retained a precarious hold in an area where the factories of Paisley increasingly replaced traditions of craftsmanship elsewhere. It would not be fair, however, to represent Paisley shawls as bereft of aesthetic qualities. The products of early industrialization have their own charm, but one that gave a pert slap in the face to all that had gone before.

EDINBURGH

At least as early as 1793, prizes were being given in Edinburgh for shawls 'in imitation of the Indian'. Artistic standards were unusually high, thanks to the foundation in 1760 of an academy 'to promote or improve designs or patterns for linen and cotton and flowered muslin manufacturers' and others, later including shawl making.[17] The results, as in France where attention to design was far commoner than in Britain, are clearly visible in the outstandingly beautiful border ends shown in fig. 46, from a shawl thought to date from about 1805–15. The shawl is remarkable for the delicacy of its colours, which was, indeed, a trait that distinguished the Edinburgh shawls as a whole from the harsher colours prevalent among Paisley shawls. The closeness in spirit

46   End border of a long shawl, 8 × 14 in., Messrs Gibb and Macdonald, Edinburgh, c. 1805–15. The absence of side borders and the shawl's unusual dimensions (in contrast to those of Paisley, where the length was twice the width), gave it something of the appearance of being handmade, and so brought it closer in spirit to the original kashmirs.

of this Edinburgh shawl to the original *kashmirs* may also be ascribed to the use of a drawloom. At the same time, there is a distinctly Scottish contribution in the depiction of the cones, which are a perfect marriage of naturalism and subtle stylization.

Although Edinburgh shawls went into decline as a result of commercial competition from nearby Paisley, a few very fine shawls continued to be manufactured until 1847. The shawl shown here was made about 1835 by

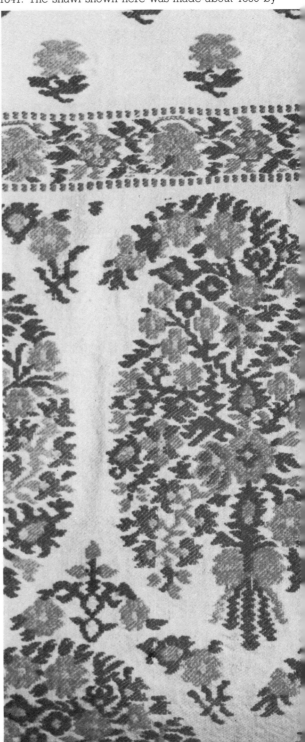

47   *Kirking shawl, 56 × 46 in., Messrs Gibb and Macdonald, Edinburgh, c. 1835. The shawl is a good example of the 'typical Edinburgh style'. Although woven in one piece, the faithful rendering of the cone, together with the subtle and harmonious shades, evokes the genuine* kashmirs.

48   *Border of a fillover shawl, Norwich, c. 1825. Against* ▷ *the characteristic cream ground, there is a closely defined, but spacious, floral design.*

Messrs Gibb and Macdonald, whose characteristically dark shawls reflect the sombre colour of the warp they used. It is an excellent example of an early 'turn-over' shawl. (By reversing the cones in two of the four side borders, they faced symmetrically to left and right when the shawl, as was fashionable about that time, was folded diagonally to allow two corners to hang more or less flush down the back.)[18] It is very likely that this 'turn-over' was also a 'kirking' shawl. Particularly fashionable in Scotland in the 1830s, kirking shawls were normally long woven or printed shawls with deep cone-filled borders, as here, and plain white or pastel centres. The colours of the borders were in suitably sober shades or sometimes in pastel. This accounted for the trade name, 'pale-ends'. It was *de rigueur* in respectable circles for the Scottish bride to wear a kirking shawl to the service on the first Sunday after her marriage, and again after the birth of the first child. These kirking shawls were very often

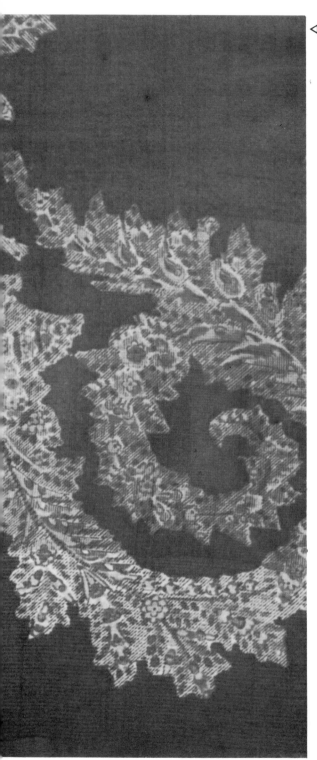

◁ 49 *Leno shawl, Messrs Towler and Campin, Norwich, c. 1850. This firm was known for the precision and delicacy of its designs, made possible by printing them on a very fine silk gauze.*

wedding presents and were among the most prized items of the bride's trousseau.[19]

NORWICH

Norwich was uniquely well placed to lead the early shawl industry in nineteenth-century Britain. Textile crafts had flourished in the city for hundreds of years, while it was sufficiently close to the busy east coast, and by sea to London, to facilitate the import of the original *kashmir* models, so fashionable in the capital at the turn of the eighteenth century. As stated already, Edward Barrow in 1784 is generally acknowledged to be the first British manufacturer of shawls.[20]

By 1802, Norwich could boast twelve manufacturers of shawls; all the shawls, it seems, were embroidered by hand. At about that date, however, a drawloom was used to weave the design directly on to the shawls. The new type of shawl was called a fillover, because 'in the weaving the face of the shawl is downward, and all the work comprising the figure is filled over it. This may be taken to mean that on the "wrong" side details of the pattern were obscured or "filled over" by floating wefts.'[21] A fine example of the border of such a fillover shawl, dating from about 1825, can be seen in fig. 48. The delightful texture, which comes across so well in the photograph, was achieved through the harmonious combination of silk and wool – very much a Norwich speciality. 'Generally,' explains Miss Clabburn, the foremost authority on Norwich shawls, 'a silk warp was used with one of a variety of wools for the weft, or else the shawl was spun of silk but whatever yarns were used for the ground, the fillover was always wool.'[22]

Towards the middle of the century, competition, particularly with Paisley, induced some of the Norwich shawl manufacturers to cut costs by replacing woven with printed designs. Despite the inevitable lowering of standards, the Norwich manufacturers succeeded in partly retrieving the situation by ensuring that the imprint was made on specially suitable muslin surfaces and also, in the example in fig. 49, on leno, which had a particularly tight weave.

The Great Exhibition of 1851 popularized the burnous, a semi-circular wrap worn by Tunisians and other tribesmen in the desert. The garment which gave protection in Africa against sand and sun appealed to

Victorian ladies for quite different reasons: the pyramidal shape made it an excellent adjunct to the wide crinoline skirts of the 1850s and 1860s. The burnous was valued also for its oriental flavour, rendered so much in vogue by the Romantics and by the increased interest among the British in the Empire that had been acquired supposedly 'in a fit of absent-mindedness'. Whatever the precise reasons, the burnous was to be seen everywhere; particularly, perhaps, in the United States, where it was a favourite garment of theatre-goers.[23]

At the time of the Industrial Revolution it was a great achievement for Norwich to retain its primacy in quality right up to the 1870s, when the change in the shape of women's dresses brought about a temporary eclipse in the fashion for shawls. A fine example, dating from around 1870, can be seen in fig. 51. Imbued in every sinuous line with the spirit of the nascent Art Nouveau movement, it seems to hold out new hope for the future.

SPITALFIELDS

The advent of the shawl brought a last-minute reprieve to Spitalfields and other centres of silk manufacture. The change in women's dresses from heavy formal attire to the muslin chemise in the late eighteenth century had caused a devastating recession in the silk industry. The manufacturers were more fortunate in Britain than across the Channel, in that an admixture of silk was necessary to give woollen thread sufficient strength to bear the stresses of production in the type of drawloom used. The spur to survival undoubtedly hastened the development of lighter silk materials, more suited to enhance the period's 'sculptural' look.

Scarves and shawls made entirely from silk became fashionable from about 1809.[24] Spitalfields silk in particular became highly prized. An exquisite Spitalfields silk shawl, dated about 1810–20, is in the collection of the Victoria & Albert Museum (see colour plate 4). Although the traditional cone motif appears, the flowers themselves have an English look about them, as if they had come out of an herbaceous border.

Although Spitalfields provided much of the inspiration for the silk industry, and was, indeed, to have an important influence on Paisley through the emigration of much of its workforce there, the attribution of silk shawls – and even of shawls as a whole – to particular centres, remains a thorny subject. The sophisticated design of the

50 Burnous, Norwich, c. 1850. The garment, which is semicircular in shape with mock hood and tassels, has a cream woollen ground with black silk flower embroidery.

51 Border of a shawl, Messrs Clabburn, Son and ▷ Crisp, Norwich, c. 1860. The shawl was plaid size and woven entirely in silk. The large elongated cones in 'scissor' pattern seem to presage Art Nouveau.

52 Long narrow striped shawl, c. 1811. The clean shiny finish was achieved by using a gauze weave with extra firming at the selvedges.

54 Photograph of a lady wearing a large shawl of black silk lace, of Spanish type, 1863. This shawl has a pattern of stylized flowers, reflecting a return to the historical style of the seventeenth century, and is particularly reminiscent of the Lady in a Mantilla by Velázquez (see fig. 13).

53 Tulle shawl, English, c. 1820. This tulle shawl was the ideal accompaniment to the embroidered cream-coloured dress, also of tulle, over a silk undergown of the same colour. Romantic feeling is enhanced by the satin trimmings on the short puffy sleeves and skirt of the dress.

shawl shown in fig. 52, therefore, cannot be ascribed to Spitalfields with any confidence. It could even have been manufactured on the Continent, although the 'Regency stripe' seems to make it exceptionally well suited to England, a point reinforced by the appearance of rather similar ones in the Lady's Magazine of 1811. This one, of about the same date, has a silk warp alternating with maroon–brown wool and cream silk weft.[25]

55 Imitation Chantilly lace shawl, c. 1850-65. The
1850s and 1860s saw a vogue for lace shawls, particularly
those of Chantilly, which were patronized by the
Empress Eugénie. Machine-made 'Chantilly' was often
of such a high standard that it was hard to distinguish
from the original.

56 White muslin shawl, 27 × 100 in. Coggeshall,
c. 1840-60. This shawl has its borders and ends
tamboured in a spot pattern, with an inner border
design of field flowers. ▷

57 Queen Victoria and Prince Albert arriving at Tréport on 2 September 1843, *by Eugène Lami, 1843. Queen Victoria is shown helping to revive the flagging Paisley shawl industry by wearing one on her person, an example followed by ladies in her entourage.*

Around 1820 tulle was popular, often embellished with a delicate floral pattern, as in the magnificent example in fig. 53, from the Gallery of English Costume at Platt Hall. As can be seen, this almost unbelievably delicate and diaphanous shawl does not so much complete, as justify, the model's delightfully Romantic dress.

Particularly fashionable in the 1860s were transparent black silk shawls, which were draped to form a satisfying contrast with white or light-coloured crinolines beneath. British manufacturers were shameless in pirating designs from other countries. Spanish lace, voluminous and heavy, was especially popular. Chantilly lace could also be plagiarized with some technical facility, as fig. 55 shows.

Embroidered shawls also enjoyed great popularity. A very successful manufactory was located at Coggeshall, a town in Essex. It was famous for its tambour embroidery on net. This cottage industry was founded in the early nineteenth century by a French or Flemish refugee called Draygo. He showed the cottagers how to stretch net on oblong embroidery frames and then how to work the design with a tambour hook.

PAISLEY

Any shawl with a cone motif – by far the commonest to be found – is still often referred to as 'Paisley'. This sweeping disregard for some half-dozen European centres which also made frequent use of the cone in their designs, contains a basic truth. In purely quantitative terms, Paisley's production amounted to far more than all the rest put together.[26] Only a relatively small number of shawls were directed towards the fashionable, while the overwhelming majority were destined for a mass market. This large-scale production enabled Paisley to undersell its competitors and virtually drive them out of business: first Edinburgh, in the 1840s, and then Norwich, in the 1860s. Typical was the complaint of the Norwich weavers to a government commission that 'they no sooner designed and marketed a shawl at considerable expense, than Paisley would, within a few weeks, be selling imitations of it at half the price'.[27] While others complained Paisley prospered, apparently without so much as a twinge of conscience.

58 *Reversible shawl, Paisley, c. 1865. All previous* ▷ *shawls bore the pattern on one side only, while the other had a confused medley of colours where the cropping machine had cut superfluous threads. The new shawls, which were completely, or almost, square, could be worn with either side showing.*

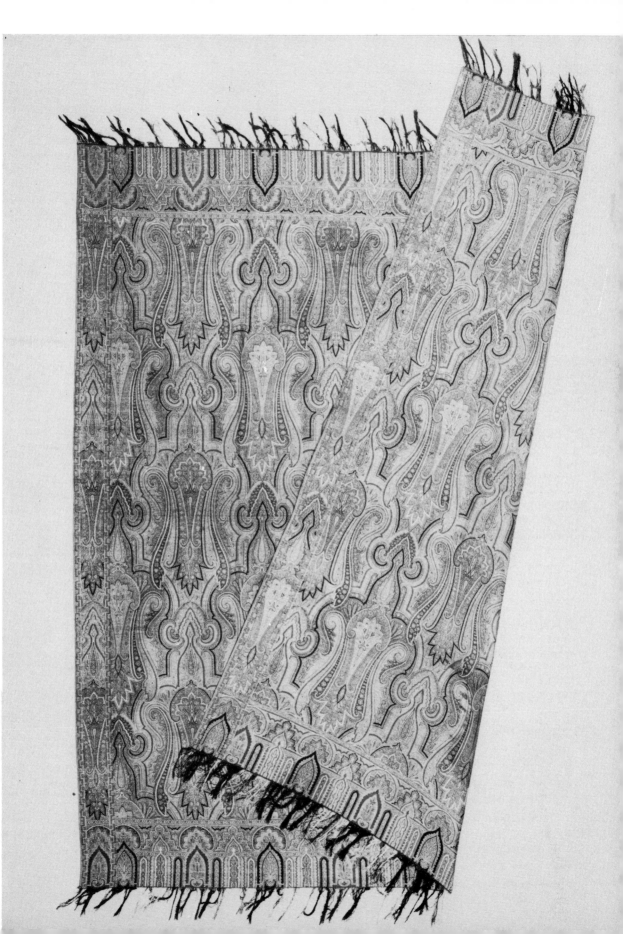

By the 1840s Paisley was a household name for shawls. It was entirely fitting, therefore, that when the industry was hit by recession, Queen Victoria should have come to its rescue. In 1842 the Queen purchased 17 Paisley shawls and promised to wear one at the forthcoming royal christening of the Prince of Wales, the future King Edward VII. Shortly afterwards, in 1843, Queen Victoria on her state visit to France again dressed as the promoter of Paisley's shawls. 'Queen Victoria', related the *Illustrated London News*, 'wore a dress of champagne-coloured silk with a green woven Paisley shawl.'[28] The splendour of the occasion – or, perhaps, the shawl – inspired Eugène Lami, depictor of the imperial court of Napoleon III, to paint the reception of the Queen at Tréport, near Cherbourg. Royal services to Paisley also included the loan of the royal *kashmirs* to the Paisley copyists. The Queen was in a particularly strong position to oblige the Paisley manufacturers after the Treaty of Lahore in March 1846, which laid down an annual tribute from the Maharajah Gholab Singh that included 12 shawl-goats and 3 pairs of shawls.[29]

The 'Chinese Fairy Tale' plaid of *c.* 1840–50 is a good example of Paisley design at its most inventive and attractive (see colour plate 5). Unlike Couder's 'Nou-Rouz' design at the French exhibition of 1839, the 'Chinese Fairy Tale' is admirably suited for a shawl, as opposed to a carpet. With the accent on pleasure (pagoda scenes and exotic vegetation), vanity (peacocks), and above all intimate domestic scenes, it is beautifully suited for feminine attire. Even the Jacquard loom's technical virtuosity, which could all too easily become an end in itself, serves just the right dreamy fantasy. In its sinuous lines and arabesques the shawl also seems to herald Art Nouveau, of which nearby Glasgow was to be one of the great European centres.

Although Paisley could cater for the luxury market far better than is commonly thought, the manufacturers were primarily concerned to exploit the mass market. One of their outstanding achievements in this field was the wholesale production of the 'reversible shawl' in the 1860s. Again, it was very much in keeping with the Paisley tradition that the idea itself was pirated from the Norwich firm of W.H. Clabburn, who had patented it in 1854 and exhibited it at the Paris Exhibition the following year.[30] The 'reversible shawl' was quite simply a shawl 'without a wrong side, the pattern identical on both sides'.[31] As for the technical process, it is best described by the acknowledged authority on the Kashmir shawl:

59   Caricature from Punch, *26 September 1857. Large shawls alone were equal to covering the capacious crinolines which had appeared the previous year.*

60   Chinese silk shawl, Canton, c. 1850–70. This shawl, ▷ made for the export market, is of cream silk with embroidered floral patterns and deeply knotted fringe.

The European reversibles were made on the Jacquard loom with a double set of warps, the repeat sections of the pattern being ingeniously composed so that the opposite sides of the cloth were complementary to one another. The redundant weft threads, when not engaged in the pattern on either face of the cloth, were left floating between the two surfaces.[32]

Shawls went into eclipse about 1870. Paisley was particularly badly hit when the Franco-Prussian War of 1870 closed the French market to British manufacturers. The chief blame, however, must surely lie with the change in women's fashions. The shawl had proved an admirable adjunct to the burgeoning crinolines which came into vogue around 1856. The task of covering the hooped structure, so amusingly ridiculed in *Punch*, was the despair of the designers of overcoats, and indeed seemed to fall more into the province of tent-makers! This challenge was answered perfectly by the voluminous Kashmir shawl, especially when expanded still further at Paisley to become a 'plaid'. As long as crinolines remained, the shawl was guaranteed an indispensable place in the feminine wardrobe. It was the

First Coster. "WHY, JACK ! WHAT'S ALL THAT !"
Second Do. "WELL, I CAN'T SAY ! UNLESS IT'S *FIREWORKS !*"

appearance of the bustle that caused the shawl to be banished – for a time, at least. For, clearly, no lady could flaunt her hind quarters, as fashion demanded, while wearing the traditional shawl. Hence the shameful practice of cutting up shawls into coats, often in the form of what was called a *visite*. This deplorable garment had long sleeves, and was shaped to allow the bustle to be displayed to maximum effect. As if that were insufficient desecration of the shawl, a collar and frilled edging around hem and cuffs were added.

Reports of the shawl's death, however, were much exaggerated. It was not the shawl, but the Paisley shawl, that went into irreversible decline in the 1870s. The success of Arthur Liberty's shop, which opened in Regent Street in 1875, shows that the demand for Asian shawls remained buoyant among the fashionable. Paisley's decline in the 1870s cannot be ascribed entirely to the advent of the bustle. An important subsidiary reason was dissatisfaction with the increasing vulgarity of the centre's output. Even allowing for the high standards which the Paisley manufacturers could sometimes meet, it irked the rich to see their social inferiors flaunting Kashmir shawls that looked to the untutored eye like the genuine article which they themselves might be wearing. Hence the move away from the better-known *kashmirs* to shawls from Amritsar, Tunis and especially China. Although the fine example in fig. 60, from Canton, dates from about 1850-70, Chinese shawls were if anything more popular after that time. And once the market ceased to be flooded by Paisley's imitation Kashmir shawls, the vogue for the originals returned, in the 1880s.[33] Finally, even Paisley shawls did not disappear from the face of the earth, as many people seem to have wished. Paisley plaids are much in evidence, for instance, in some of the delightful scenes which James Tissot painted in England during the 1880s and later.[34] Many of these plaids are simple tartans, far better suited to the mass market than some of the more pretentious imitations of *kashmirs*.

The nineteenth century lay under the spell of the shawl to the point where even men aspired to wear a much abridged model. In fig. 61, a French fashion plate of 1836 shows the man on the left in a *redingote*, on which he sports a shawl collar of Canadian bison. The fashion for shawl collars dated back to the time of Holbein, and was to continue into the 1830s, when the term 'roll collars' was used (although by that time they were in fact laid flat).

SCARVES AND BOAS
During the Age of the Shawl, scarves were relegated to a minor role in women's dress, although the masculine obsession with the art of tying scarves and cravats,

61   Fashion plate from the Petit Courrier des Dames, 1836. The man on the left wears a redingote with a shawl collar of Canadian bison fur.

thanks to Beau Brummell's influence, continued well into the nineteenth century. As for women's scarves, their use was revived among fashionable ladies around the 1840s and 1850s, and especially during the 1860s, when the shawl was about to go out of fashion. There was a particular interest in imitation Valenciennes lace, which was made on the Leavers machine.[35] Many of the styles at that time harked back nostalgically to the eighteenth century. Thus the fichu named after Marie-Antoinette, now seen as a tragic victim of revolutionary circumstances, was particularly fashionable. In that revival of interest the obsession of Napoleon III's Empress Eugénie with the cult of Marie-Antoinette may well have played a part.

5 'Chinese Fairy Tale' plaid, Paisley, *c.* 1840–50. Paisley is so often associated with mass production that some of its finest shawls for fashionable wear risk being overlooked. The manufacture of this enchanting plaid was a remarkable technical feat that is thought to have required no less than 150,000 shots of weft and 180 warps per square inch of an enormous area.

6 Fashion plate from the *Gazette du Bon Ton*, May 1913. The model, depicted by the painter and fashion illustrator, H. Robert Dammy, wears 'the garden party ensemble' of Jacques Doucet, the famous couturier and art collector. The artist's delicate flower style evokes the movement and freedom of Art Nouveau, especially in the long serpentine 'Empire' scarf in soft rose tones.

7 Fashion plate from the *Journal des Dames et des Modes*, 1913. Georges Barbier provides here a spectacular demonstration of the affinities between fashion and the fine arts. The sharp geometric outline of the blue velvet sash, weighted with pearl tassels, serves perfectly both to reinforce the Art Deco lines of the model's dress and to anchor her in the Art Deco colours of her environment.

8 'Peacock Feather' silk scarf, Messrs Liberty of London, 1975. Originally designed by Rex Silver, *c.* 1900, this delightful motif in subtle tones of green, cream and turquoise was reprinted for Liberty's centenary year.

62   Imitation Valenciennes lace scarf, Nottingham,
1843. Made on the Leavers machine, this lace scarf
reproduces the delicate patterns found on late
eighteenth- and early nineteenth-century Valenciennes
lace. This example has picot edging which has been
sewn on.

63 *Marie-Antoinette fichu, fashion plate from* Harper's Bazar, *15 May 1869. The fichu, worn by the two standing ladies, is larger and heavier than forerunners in the eighteenth century. It was usually trimmed with fine lace or ribbon and fastened in front.*

The boa, as it appeared in Debucourt's print of 1800, still lacked many of the accessory's characteristic features. If rounded and made of fur, its short length and narrow girth, and above all its failure to grip its wearer in a tight embrace, shows that it marks only the first, if an important, stage in the boa's development. Perhaps it should still be styled a 'stole', especially as the word 'boa' does not appear to have been current before 1829.[36] Debucourt's drawing does much to explain the accessory's shape and the way it was worn. The presence of the Directory furniture is a useful reminder of the interrelationship between dress and interior decoration at the time. The straight line of the stole is the obvious complement to that of the desk, over which the lady leans as she ponders her reply to the *billet doux* she has just received. The straight lines of her own elongated figure also show that stoles were sill being worn straight, with the obvious intention of enhancing the linear effect.

64 Réponse au Billet *by Ph.-L. Debucourt, 1800. The boa seems to have made its first unobtrusive appearance in dark fur in this engraving.*

The boa, alone, however, was in any position to dispute primacy with the shawl, and then only for a short time at the beginning, and again towards the end, of the period. By 1805 the long white boa had already made its appearance. The English fashion plate in fig. 65 shows a lady in full dress clasping one to her. Her ample *décolletage* explains the accessory's practical and coquettish use. At one and the same time it provided protection from the cold and served to frame the generous area exposed. Another virtue of the boa was

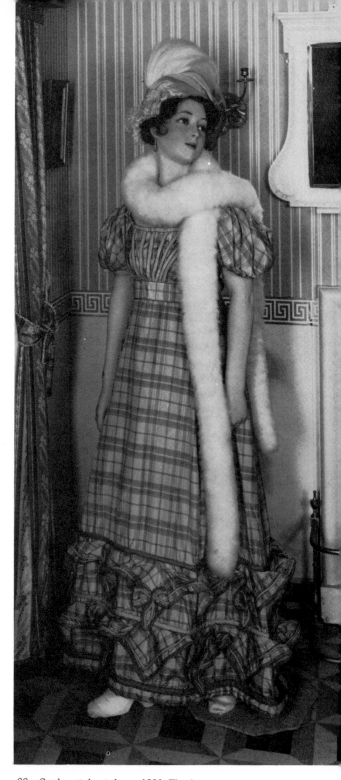

65 Boa, English fashion plate, 1805. The light white fur boa, at first reserved for formal wear, came so much into vogue that it was adopted for outdoor attire as well.

66 Snake-style stole, c. 1820. The boa, as worn here, helps to emphasize the vertical lines in the smocking of the bodice.

the way in which its curve around the neck echoed the shape of the coiffure, and the bend in the white plumes that were so fashionable. The boa was far less suitable for walking dress, because social convention restricted the size of both *décolletage* and the plumed coiffure.

Mlle Rivière's portrait by Ingres illustrates the romantic enchantment of the white snake-like stole for its wearers. As it writhes around her body it seems every inch a boa, made in fact of white fox fur, which would again be a favourite accessory with Poiret in the twentieth century (see fig. 70). The white boa shows better than anything else in the portrait the intimate rapport between the Antique and Romantics. While Mlle Rivière is clothed in a neo-classical chemise, its sculptural quality is offset by the gathered shoulders and sleeves, and more especially by the luxuriant curves of the boa itself. As if to drive that point home, the severity of the lady's coiffure is in sharp contrast to the delicate, almost troubadour cast of the landscape behind her. That may well explain the lure of long ermine stoles for the Empress Josephine, herself a keen patron of *le style troubadour*. Ermine as the royal material *par excellence* gave such stoles added social cachet.[37]

It was hardly surprising that by the 1820s the white stole seems to have become a little *trop de trop* – the victim of its own extravagant pretensions. That is certainly the impression conveyed by a carefully researched re-creation in the Costume Museum at Bath. Both the gleaming white stole and the rich dress of apricot taffeta belong to the beginning of the 1820s. The boa seems to detract from the dress itself. It covers up the attractive *décolletage*, instead of drawing attention to it, as the elaborate smocking around the bust was intended to do. The boa also serves to link the elaborate top and bottom of the dress, while the plain middle section, in fact, provides a pleasing contrast to both.

As if to defy logic, a strange variant of the boa did, nonetheless, gain wide currency in the middle of the century. The 'victorine', named after Queen Victoria, was a kind of tippet, lined with quilted silk and tied in front with two short ends.[38] It was often made of velvet and lined with padded silk, and was complemented with a matching muff. The victorine's popularity seems to have owed little to its own qualities, and almost everything to the Great Exhibition of 1851 which served to launch it.

The boa which enlivened the neo-classical line was in a sense the victim of its own success. The burgeoning crinolines and bustle, which carried the rebellion to the point of changing the fashions altogether, also removed the opportunity for wearing boas or stoles. The accessory therefore went into abeyance, until the appearance of a slim line around 1870 provided a

THE GREAT BOA TIPPET 1829
Still we have predilection for the Serpent

67 The Great Boa Tippet, by William Heath, 1829. *This modern Medea in 1829, when the early Romantic painters, writers and musicians were reaching their crescendo, shows how the boa, along with inflated Renaissance sleeves and vast beribboned hats, came to symbolize Romanticism in dress.*

suitable opportunity for the boa's re-emergence in the 1880s and 1890s. A delightful dress appeared in the Paris autumn collections of 1898, in crêpe de Chine with black chenille polka dots, especially at the bottom, revealing the lace underskirt with its curving patterns. The whole style of the dress, not to mention the décor around the model, hints at the emergence of Art Nouveau. It was as a fashion accessory to this style that the boa was to figure so prominently in the next century.

68 *'Paris model from Autumn Reception Costume',
fashion plate from Harper's Bazar, 17 September 1898.
This unusual boa is of white silk plissé, shirred into
ruffles at regular intervals. The horizontal lines are*
echoed by the large white mousseline de soie *bow-tie
and scarf-belt, which has been pulled tight to satisfy
the period's obsession with slender waists.*

4

Search for a New Identity

1900–1980

Contemporaries have always been perplexed by the fashions of their own time, and the author must admit to being no exception. Perhaps in years to come the fashions of the twentieth century will yield up their secrets to the inquiries of the dress historian. Yet, on the face of it, contradictions and uncertainties beset almost every area of life, and taste above all. Fashion by its nature is élitist, yet society professes to be democratic. Does that in part account for the heady, but furtive, pursuit of fashion in our own day? On any but the most formal occasion, people today often appear to be competing in degrees of undress. How can dustman be distinguished from duke, except that the latter is likely to be less formally dressed? In the sixteenth century it would have been called 'the World turned upside down'; today many take it as a mark of good taste, for anti-fashion is itself highly fashionable. Perhaps it would be truer to say, however, that as society has fragmented, different fashions have been followed by different groups. The only common bond that may sometimes be seen is the expression of a certain individualism, yet, until quite recently, the widespread wearing of blue jeans seemed to cast doubt on the reliability of even that modest generalization.

If fashion is in process of dissolution today, it does seem easier to discern nearer to the beginning of the twentieth century. While before the First World War the 'certainties' inherited from the nineteenth century may have begun to crumble, the outward forms, especially as exemplified by dress, remained largely intact. It was only in the wake of the Second World War that fashion as it used to exist seemed to melt away.

The twentieth century, as far as shawls, stoles and scarves are concerned, has tended to move increasingly towards informality, despite frequent yearnings for the return to a more formal past. Stoles, usually in the form of the boa, predominated in the early years of the century, doubtless because they were seen to epitomize formality, while scarves have tended to be worn in the more relaxed conditions of today. As for shawls, they appear, as often in the past, to have been associated with movements of a more or less Romantic kind.

FUR AND FEATHERED BOAS

Fashionable ladies entered the twentieth century embraced by their boas. Without them women would hardly have been dressed to fit decoratively, as society demanded, into the world of Art Nouveau. The fashionable silhouette in 1900 comprised close-fitting sleeves, an even tighter waist, and a pronounced accentuation of the bust, with skirts tight over the hips and flaring out below to produce what was called the 'S-bend'. The sinuous curves of the boa enhanced this style to create a reflection of Art Nouveau itself.

In 1900 the Exposition Universelle in Paris by its magnificent display of furs decreed that fur should be used for boas and other types of stole. Already in 1893 the highly popular Franco-Russian alliance, with the visit of the Russian fleet to Toulon, had done much to encourage the use of fur.[1] Although sable was undoubtedly the favoured fur, ermine, mink, skunk, marten and many other kinds were also worn. Such was the enthusiasm for fur that stoles often reached almost to the ankles, while ladies delighted to sport the heads, tails and paws of their spoils.

The feather boa became popular around 1904, and went far to atone for the lapse of good taste among some of the wearers of fur. In England credit for relaunching the fashion has been attributed traditionally to the patronage of Queen Alexandra, although a writer of the period noted, 'it is not everyone who can boast the swan-like throat of our graceful Queen, to which a full fluffy adornment is particularly suitable'.[2] In France the fashion for feathered boas owed much to the support of Mme Paquin. In *Paquin à cinq heures* Henri Gervex provides a fascinating view of the interior of her fashion house. It is noticeable there that the boas no longer hug their wearers in a serpentine embrace, but are allowed to hang loosely and gracefully from their shoulders and arms. The luxurious dreamy quality of the feather boa has probably never been rendered more beautifully than by Klimt in his portrait of Hermine Gallia in 1904. If the portrait hardly seems to resemble a fashion plate, then appearances are misleading. The sitter was the wife of Moritz Gallia, a leading patron of the Wiener

Werkstätte, Vienna's avant-garde design group. It was Klimt's practice to insist that his sitters wore a dress specially designed by the Werkstätte.

1912 will always be remembered in the history of dress for the introduction by Poiret of the white fox stole. It was deceptively simple in design, but the design was everything. The stole's design can be best understood in relation to what Laver calls 'a fundamental change . . . in feminine dress in the year 1910'. Women, in effect, were liberated from their tight corsets to the extent that their breasts were freed and their waists less tightly constrained. In short, women were released from their imprisonment in the S-shape and allowed to stand upright for the first time in a decade.[3] The result, in aesthetic terms, was to allow the gentle curves of the feminine form renewed expression. The white fox stole by its downy texture was admirably suited to do this, as was the cylindrical muff that sometimes accompanied it. A further refinement was the addition of fur trimmings to

69 Hermine Gallia, by Gustav Klimt, 1904. The feathered boa admirably softens the angularity of the silhouette.

70 Fashion plate from the Journal des Dames et des ▷ Modes, 1912. Poiret's white fox stole is contrasted with his other creation, the famous 'minaret gown', in which the black velvet dress is tiered with silk muslin, trimmed with the fur of skunks.

1.U.S.

2.U.S.

3.U.S.

4.U.S.

5.U.S.

6.U.S.

◁ 71 *'Smart Boas for Spring Wear', advertisement by Messrs Swan and Edgar Ltd, 1916. 1. 'Marabout and Ostrich Feather Collar . . . 8/6'. 2. 'Ostrich Feather Ruffle with Satin Bow . . . 12/9'. 3. 'Ostrich and Marabout Feather Cravat . . . 17/9'. 4. 'Marabout and Ostrich Collar, finished Oxidised or Gilt Button . . . 25/6'. 5. Flat Ostrich Feather Ruffle, made of two strands, finished Satin and Feather Rosette . . . 18/9'. 6. Full Ostrich Feather Ruffle . . . 31/6'.*

the dress. That had been done before, but in this case the fur was so positioned to give the illusion of the dress floating upwards. Illusion was, indeed, largely the source of the appeal of the white fox stole and its accompaniments, for the stole was inspired by the *Ballet Russe*. Diaghilev revelled in orientalism and the furs, as well as the silks, it evoked.[4] And afterwards the white fox stole created its own legend of glamour and innocence – strangely enhanced when appropriated by the early film stars.

Boas and furs from the 1914 war onwards enjoyed enormous popularity, while inflicting a blow against good taste that even the Victorians could seldom match. Fig. 71 shows Swan and Edgar's 'Smart Boas for Spring Wear'. It would be pleasant to record an improvement over the next few decades, but if anything aesthetic standards seem to have sunk still lower. 'Common in the 1930s and 1940s ', writes Alison Lurie in *The Language of Clothes*, 'was the wearing around the neck of one or more animal skins (usually fox, sometimes mink) complete with legs, tails and head – with the sharp little teeth bared, the glass eyes beady. It is not clear whether the fox or mink represented the animal nature of the woman who wore it, or whether it was a kind of trophy representing the man or men she had captured, hung round the neck in the primitive manner, as in some portraits of Diana the Huntress.'[5] In either case, a man would have been wise to keep his distance. From this nadir new and more attractive styles developed in the late 1940s. On the one hand women took to wearing voluminous fur capes, which gave them a bizarre top-heavy look, but one which could be flattering to their breasts. Another development initiated by Princess Elizabeth at her wedding in 1947 was the reintroduction of a long white fox stole, accompanied by a fur-lined blue cape.

From the 1950s the emphasis has been on experiment – what Elizabeth Ewing in her book on *Fur in Dress* has called 'an increasing search for something different', while *Harper's Bazar* was to trumpet desperately, 'The shape's the thing'. And in the 1960s the President of Bergdorf Goodman echoed the same sentiments in a

speech: 'Regarding furs, for example: think back . . . remember the mass-produced mink stole of which millions were sold in the USA. Now the outstanding characteristic is not the sameness but the difference in shape, colour and treatment of skins.'[6]

After seventy years of largely unsuccessful experimentation, it is hardly surprising that some designers favour a return to the boa. A fine example of a white fox stole appeared on a Bill Blass evening dress of around 1970, while the boa style was still being popularized by Yves Saint-Laurent in the 1980s.[7]

SHAWLS

By the twentieth century the Antique, India and Spain had ensured a permanent place for the shawl in the fashionable lady's wardrobe. Although from time to time shawls might be forgotten, they would always be rediscovered with cries of incredulous delight.

The silver gauze shawl in fig. 72 proves, whatever some have said, that Indian shawls were alive and well in the early twentieth century. Although the shawl departs somewhat from tradition in being woven with a butterfly motif, the borders, ends and corners of the central panel all bear the immemorial cone design.

On the eve of the First World War the new popularity of knitted wool brought to high fashion whole knitted coats and even suits, recommended for sporting and motoring wear and for country weekends. Naturally, the shawl, too, was assigned a place in this mass conversion. Shetland wool and patterns were in particularly keen demand, especially after Gordon Selfridge had made them more widely known among the general public by arranging a knitting and spinning demonstration by Shetlanders in his Oxford Street store.[8]

As Art Nouveau dissolved into Art Deco, the shawl seems to have been called into play to heighten the exotic effect so popular at the time, and to provide luxuriant curves to complement the over-severe vertical lines of what was still an essentially sculptural look. The black net shawl in fig. 73 illustrates this new trend. The *Gazette du Bon Ton* in June 1914 showed a lady described as dressed in a Kashmir shawl, though one with a very uncharacteristic fur trimming that had recently become highly fashionable. Even if the means is questioned, the outcome is surely deliciously oriental, especially in the effect created by the very long sleeves.

While Art Deco held sway in the 1920s and 1930s, shawls once again became highly fashionable, together with long scarves. They brought much-needed relief to the plain outline of tubular chemise dresses. As the influence of Poiret and the *Ballet Russe* receded, the taste for orientalia remained and became more diffused. No garment was suited to express this taste for the

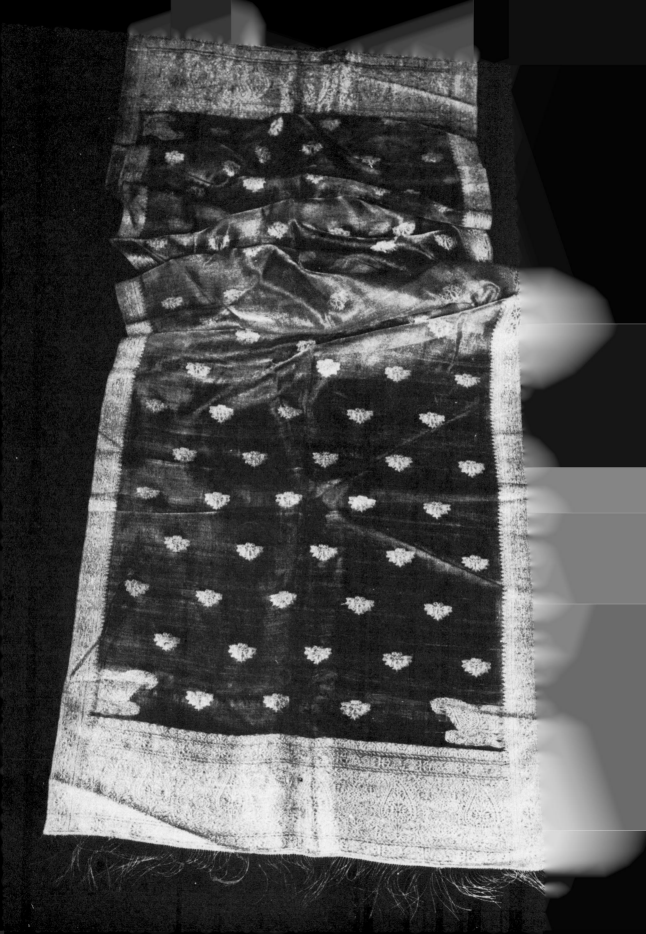

72 Indian shawl, 21 × 92 in., c. 1900. The shawl shows
how far India went to satisfy the tastes of its Western
clientele. The realistic rendering of a parade of
butterflies on a silver gauze textile mirrored European
taste. The borders alone, with the traditional cone
design, were true to Indian traditions.

73 Black net shawl, 25 × 96 in., c. 1910–20. This shawl,
tamboured in cream cotton with spot design, and with a
deep border at either end of curving geometric patterns
and floral motifs, and enriched with steel beads,
provides a good example of early Art Deco.

74 Black silk crêpe shawl, 52 in. sq, c. 1920–30. This ▷
Art Deco shawl is machine-embroidered in a large
pattern of stylized roses in vivid pink, orange, magenta,
blue and brown, and is lined in orange velvet.

oriental in more acceptable terms than the shawl and
kindred garments. 'The increasingly lean silhouettes of
the 1920s,' in the evocative words of Mrs Baines, 'were
flattened and softened by the voluminous kimono-type
overcoats and wraps, burnouses and shawls.' She goes
on to note that Chinese shawls were often so large and
with such deep fringes that they enveloped the wearer
from neck to toe. These shawls were embroidered with
such bright flowers that the auditoriums of London
theatres began to resemble herbaceous borders.[9] Bold
floral motifs were a major theme of shawls (see fig. 74).
As an alternative, but creating much the same general
effect, were the fine Spanish shawls or *mantons de
Manilla*, revived again after their popularity in the
nineteenth century.

In recent years shawls have tended to be in eclipse,
interspersed with some scintillating revivals. The famous
Norwich shawls continued to be made in small numbers
by Messrs Grout and Company until the 1930s. They
were printed and made of China crêpe. Afterwards a
small Jacquard woven shawl, 45 inches long by 30 inches
wide, was made by Messrs Hindes, until 'the last
handloom,' in Miss Clabburn's words, 'was given
honourable retirement in the Bridewell Museum,
Norwich'.[10]

The 1970s may be described as the peasants' decade.
From Mexico to Yugoslavia, from Poland to Austria, the
colourful dress of peasants was everywhere raided to

75 *Fashion photograph of a peasant shawl, designed by Frank Usher, 1972. Peasant or 'ethnic' shawls popularized by, among others, Yves Saint-Laurent, were often worn in the 1970s.*

brighten the wardrobes of Europe's sophisticates. One of these 'peasantist' shawls was designed by Frank Usher in 1972 (fig. 75). An adaptation of the poncho, described as a shawl, was advertised for beach wear in the spring of 1977. It was made in black cotton with large floral motifs in vivid colours, and created by Jules-François Crahay for Lanvin.[11] The 1980s has seen a revival of shawls worn outdoors over coats and dresses. Liberty's printed shawls have become very fashionable. Her Majesty Queen Elizabeth II charmed many in the United States by wearing a blue and white-flecked shawl over her matching dress during her visit there in 1983.

SCARVES

Scarves, of rich lace, filmy gauze or embroidered muslin, often completed the outdoor attire of Edwardian ladies. The period's nostalgia made the 'Empire' scarf a particular favourite (see colour plate 6). True to the originals, they were sometimes so long that they were akin to stoles, and were, indeed, often worn as alternatives to boas. Like the latter, they were usually draped loosely around shoulders and arms. A tulle scarf tied beneath the chin was also often used to secure a broad-brimmed hat. The ends of the various scarves were almost always allowed to fall loose, often streaming out behind the wearer. Fluttering scarves, unfurled parasols and billowing muslin dresses sometimes caused fashionable women to be compared with ships in full sail.

Edwardian women in their voluminous drapery also evoked the Orient, a source of inspiration that went back to at least the turn of the century. With the arrival of the *Ballet Russe* in Paris in 1909, the vogue for orientalia became an unbridled passion. Diaghilev's orgiastic dancers, in the bold primary colours of Léon Bakst's costumes, burst through the period's debilitating sentimentality, expressed so aptly in its shapeless clothing and anaemic pastel shades, to liberate a stunned and exhilarated public. After ballets, especially *Schéhérazade*, which 'exploded like a sun-burst or rainbow' in 1910, attitudes, and above all those expressed in dress, were transformed.[12]

Paul Poiret was the undisputed interpreter of the *Ballet Russe* and the vogue for orientalism in the incestuous world of haute couture. Besides echoing the designs and colours of Bakst, he went straight to the oriental sources themselves. Around 1910 he is reported to have 'visited the Victoria & Albert Museum and made a careful study of a group of turbans in the Indian Section'. Within weeks his copies were selling well in Paris.[13] Poiret, however, might have remained just one among several leaders of fashion, had he not possessed a quite remarkable flair for publicity. He established himself on the eve of the First World War as leader – or more precisely, sultan – in a circle that brought together some of the most prominent people in society and the arts. His authority was put beyond challenge by his famous party, the 'Thousand and Second Night', a Persian festival, at which he received his 300 distinguished guests in caftan and bejewelled white silk

76 Cover from Vogue, *1 July 1918. This fashion magazine advocated a return to soft, feminine garments and accessories, such as the* buffons *and fichus of the late eighteenth century.*

turban. Later that evening Poiret was to fling open the cage-door of his harem to release his 'favourite concubine', Mme Poiret, dressed in harem pantaloons, tunic and turban. Turbans were, indeed, one of his great specialities as a couturier. Painstaking research, as well as considerable artifice, went into designing them. He imported fabrics specially from the Middle and Far East, while always keeping in mind the Persian miniatures he had seen at the Victoria & Albert Museum.[14] Paul Poiret gave the scarf an exciting and important role in what has been aptly called his Hellenic Style. He wrote:

> While studying sculptures of ancient times, I learned to use one point of support, the shoulders, where before me it had been the waist. All my gowns flared from the point of support at the extremity of the shoulders and were never fastened at the waist. This new basic principle caused fashion to evolve toward classical antiquity . . . Fabrics flowed from this ideal point like water from a fountain and draped the body in a way that was entirely natural.[15]

The result was a reinterpretation of antiquity by a sensibility steeped in Art Nouveau and the *Ballet Russe*. When contemporaries spoke of a revival of Empire fashions, they drew attention to shared preoccupations with line and drapery, but failed to distinguish between two different states of mind. Directory and Empire gowns accentuated nudity, while Poiret gave feminine charms an engagingly chaste appearance. In the dress designer's words, 'From now on breasts will no longer be "worn".'[16] Although the Greeks would have been rightly scandalized by Poiret's dictum, he undoubtedly succeeded in producing a new and enchanting style by dint of simplifying classical dress.

It was a mark of Poiret's genius that out of simplicity he and his followers charmed so many different and delightful styles. An example, tending towards traditional Art Nouveau, was the Rose Dress produced by Poiret's rival, Jacques Doucet, in 1913 (see colour plate 6). Ingenious use is made of three scarves. The enormous straw hat is anchored with a black scarf that passes beneath the chin. Around the wearer's neck is a second diminutive scarf in the form of a delightful pink bow-tie. One of the most attractive features of the ensemble is the long 'Empire' scarf, which starts at the high waist and ends draped over the right arm. The scarves play a vital part in describing the famous Art Nouveau curve, while also echoing features of the dress itself.

Far closer to Art Deco in spirit is the full evening dress in tulle and satin, with velvet sash completed by acorns in the form of pearls, drawn for the *Journal des Dames et des Modes* by Georges Barbier in the same year (see colour plate 7).

Romantic nostalgia for the past surfaced again in a revival of the late eighteenth-century fichu. In its 'Hot Weather Fashions Number' for 1 July 1918, *Vogue* featured on its cover a model wearing one made of white muslin.

If Poiret is remembered as a dress designer by the public at large, while the names of many of his rivals have been relegated to the small print in scholarly works, it is because of his close collaboration with artists, and above all Raoul Dufy. Although this painter has seldom been properly recognized outside the small circle of his devoted patrons, millions have unwittingly admired his textile designs. Dufy's earliest work was for Poiret's Martine shop. He provided delightfully naïve, but carefully executed, printing blocks to which the workforce – girls of about thirteen years of age – applied the colours. The basic aim was to express the fresh untutored vision of the young in the form of art. Poiret's choice of Dufy to direct the enterprise was inspired. His talent was essentially for decorative art, and he turned to artistic purpose more successfully than any other artist the independence of line and colour that were an almost inevitable effect of the use of woodcuts on material. As in his paintings, to which he applied the same technique with conscious intent, Dufy achieved highly attractive results from this double effect. The success of the little 'Martine factory' led to Dufy's employment between 1912 and 1928 by Bianchini-Férier, the great firm of silk weavers in Lyons.[17] As can be seen from fig. 77, many of these designs were admirably suited for scarves. This design is interesting, precisely because it is more geometric than the majority of Dufy's work. More typical was his scarf, 'The Elephants', on which blue elephants gambol amidst red flowers with green and blue leaves, among which stags bound and leopards lurk, all set against a pink background and bright-blue border. Thus the avant-garde designs of Dufy triumphed in the dress of fashionable women, who would sometimes stand as tributes to his artistry, while eloquently denouncing his canvases at art exhibitions![18]

Scarves, which attained the heights of elegance with the inspiration of Poiret and Dufy, were reduced by the rigours of the Second World War to objects of utility. That was demonstrated most clearly by the use of the triangular headscarf, popularized by the Princesses Elizabeth and Margaret, and worn to protect the hair in bad weather. A set of Mayfair scarves, advertised in September 1944, shows the extent to which elegance had succumbed to austerity, the latter practised with masochistic defiance (fig. 78). Only number 40, described as a 'woollen scarf', but in reality a shawl, exuded an air of pre-war luxury. Costing 54/- and two whole clothing coupons, it was certainly destined for a rich lady and perhaps one whose admirer was prepared to forgo his sartorial aspirations on her behalf. Both numbers 39 and 42, however, bear witness to the lingering popularity of the inter-war turban, although so reduced in size that it took, in the case of the first, one coupon, and of the second, none at all. Number 43 was a hood, which seems to have had nothing to recommend it, except that it required no coupons for its acquisition. With the exception of number 44, this is a sorry collection. The public should be grateful to Her Majesty the Queen and other ladies of the royal family for their gracious patronage of the humble triangular headscarf, the least pretentious in the collection, and the only one with some aesthetic possibilities.

77   Design for a scarf by Raoul Dufy, c. 1928. This pen and gouache study was for a silk scarf for the Lyons firm of MM. Bianchini-Férier. The geometric flowers and hard-edge abstraction anticipated many themes of abstract fabric design in subsequent decades.

What is the secret of the headscarf's popularity? What makes it the favourite attire of so many women, from princesses to charladies? In her fascinating book, *The Language of Clothes*, Alison Lurie writes eloquently of 'the large vocabulary of expressive possibilities' at the disposal of the wearers of headscarves:

> The fabric of which the scarf is made can be related to outdoor temperature, or it can be a class indicator – wool being considered aristocratic, chiffon *nouveau riche*, silk upper-middle class, cotton middle class or arty and synthetics working class. Another important consideration is the manner in which the scarf is tied, whether conventionally under the chin, exotically at the nape of the neck or on the top of the head turban or charlady style. But most significant of all, probably, is the colour and (if any) the pattern of the scarf, which . . . convey a whole range of subtle and important personal messages.[19]

Few would surely disagree with the bulk of Miss Lurie's analysis. The Hermès headscarf with its horse designs

has generally been regarded as a symbol of the English upper classes. Yet the correlation of fabric and class – doubtless intended to be tongue in cheek – surely relates to an earlier class-bound era that exists today only in the rhetoric of certain politicians. What is surely far more significant is the adoption of the headscarf across class lines. In retrospect it may well seem a more significant vehicle for democratization in dress than the ubiquitous blue jeans. And the fact that headscarves were adopted almost universally in Britain during the last war, when the population was fused together in a common national identity, speaks for itself. At the same time, the author is surely right in alluding to 'a whole range of subtle and important personal messages', which the headscarf is unusually suited to convey. Perhaps we are justified in concluding, therefore, that the search for a new identity which we posited at the start of the chapter has resulted in a far more widespread expression of individualism, within a community more socially united than in the past. Yet, sadly, democratization has undermined taste, and individualism alone has proved unable to redeem it. Perhaps society needs the stimulus of some equivalent of the *Ballet Russe*, or the genius of another Poiret or Dufy. In the meantime, it might be wise to return to some of the most entrancing models of the past, such as the 'Peacock Feather' fabric design of *c.* 1900 (see colour plate 8), revived by Liberty for their centenary scarf in 1975.

Notes

INTRODUCTION
1   *Journal des Dames et des Modes*, No. 22, 15 January 1805, p. 186.

CHAPTER 1

BORROWINGS FROM THE RENAISSANCE
1   C.W. & P. Cunnington, *Handbook of English Costume in the Seventeenth Century*, Faber & Faber 1972, p. 101
2   F. Weiss, 'Bejewelled Fur Tippets – and the Palatine Fashion', *Costume*, No. 4, 1970, p. 38.
3   *Ibid*. p. 38.
4   London, Victoria & Albert Museum, *Hollar to Heideloff: an Exhibition of Fashion Prints drawn from the Collections of Members of the Costume Society*, Costume Society, 1979, p. 7.
5   J.L. Nevinson, *The Four Seasons by Wenceslas Hollar*, Costume Society, 1979, p. 7.
6   Weiss, *op. cit*., pp. 37, 40–1.

MILITARY SASHES AND CRAVATS
7   L. Kybalová, *Encyclopédie illustrée du Costume et de la Mode*, Gründ 1976, p. 441.
8   J.L. Nevinson, 'Origin and Early History of the Fashion Plate', *U.S. National Museum Bulletin*, No. 250. Contribution from *The Museum of History and Technology*, Paper 60, Smithsonian Press, 1967, p. 82.
9   Paris, Musée de La Mode et du Costume, *Indispensables Accessoires, XVIe–XXe siècle*, 1984, pp. 13–14.
10   C.W. & P. Cunnington, *A Dictionary of English Costume*, Adam & Charles Black 1960, p. 204.

ORIENTAL INFLUENCES
11   B.B. Baines, *Fashion Revivals*, B.T. Batsford 1981, pp. 155, 186.
12   *Ibid*., p. 157.
13   M.H. Swain, 'Nightgown into Dressing Gown: a study of men's nightgowns, 18th century', *Costume*, No. 6, 1972, p. 10.
14   Baines, *op. cit*., p. 157.

15   Swain, *op. cit*., p. 11.
16   Baines, *op. cit*., p. 159.
17   F. Boucher, *20,000 Years of Fashion*, Harry N. Abrams, Inc., 1966, pp. 228, 431.

CHAPTER 2

THE 'MODEST' SCARF
1   C.W. & P. Cunnington, *Handbook of English Costume in the Eighteenth Century*, Faber & Faber 1972, p. 142.
2   *Ibid*., p. 221.
3   *Ibid*., p. 220
4   *Ibid*., pp. 75-6.
5   *Ibid*., p. 75.
6   *Ibid*., p. 221.
7   *Ibid*., p. 152.
8   *Ibid*., pp. 142, 331; C.W. & P. Cunnington, *A Dictionary of English Costume*, p. 219.
9   *The Compact Edition of the Oxford English Dictionary*, 2 Vols., Oxford University Press 1971, Vol. 2, p. 2659.
10   *Ibid*.
11   *Ibid*.
12   Cunnington, *Handbook of English Costume in the Eighteenth Century*, p. 325.
13   New York, Metropolitan Museum of Art, *The Eighteenth-Century Woman*, 1981, p. 49.
14   S. Eriksen, *Early Neo-Classicism in France*, Faber & Faber 1974, p. 50.
15   *Ibid*.
16   *Ibid*., p. 393; Plates 428 & 389.
17   A. Ribeiro, *A Visual History of Costume: The Eighteenth Century*, B.T. Batsford, 1983, p. 121.
18   Cunnington, *Handbook of English Costume in the Eighteenth Century*, p. 326.
19   Ribeiro, *op. cit*., p. 142.
20   M. Braun-Ronsdorf, *The Wheel of Fashion: Costume since the French Revolution*, Thames & Hudson 1964, p. 12.
21   E.L. Vigée-Lebrun, *Souvenirs*, 2 Vols., Charpentier et Cie., 1869, Vol. 1, p. 74.

22 Fort Worth, Kimbell Art Museum, *Elisabeth Louise Vigée-Lebrun*, 1982, p. 23, Catalogue No. 24; p. 25, Catalogue No. 28; p. 26, Catalogue No. 38; p. 35, fig. 2.
23 Vigée-Lebrun, *op. cit.*, Vol. 1, p. 37.
24 Los Angeles, County Museum of Art, *An Elegant Art*, 1983, p. 103.

FROM OLD-FASHIONED TIPPET TO NEW-FANGLED SNAKE
25 Ribeiro, *op. cit.*, p. 144.
26 Cunnington, *Handbook of English Costume in the Eighteenth Century*, pp. 142, 152–3.
27 *Ibid.*, p. 331.
28 P. Earnshaw, *A Dictionary of Lace*, Shire Publications 1982, p. 170.
29 Cunnington, *Handbook of English Costume in the Eighteenth Century*, pp. 152-3.
30 *Journal des Dames et des Modes*, No. XXVI, 22 August 1798, pp. 8–9.
31 M. Davenport, *The Book of Costume*, Crown Publishers 1972, pp. 545-6.
32 A. Ribeiro, ' "Turquerie": Turkish Dress and English Fashion in the Eighteenth Century', *Connoisseur*, Vol. 201, No. 807, May 1979, p. 17.
33 Melbourne, Victoria Art Gallery, *The Great Eighteenth-Century Exhibition*, 1982, p. 119.
34 Baines, *op. cit.*, p. 160.
35 *Ibid.*, pp. 161-2.
36 A. Buck, *Dress in Eighteenth-Century England*, B.T. Batsford 1979, p. 47.

THE SHAWL AS 'THE GIFT OF PRINCES'
37 J. Irwin, *The Kashmir Shawl*, HMSO 1973, p. 1.
38 A. Gernsheim, *Victorian and Edwardian Fashion: a photographic survey*, Dover Publications 1981, p. 30.
39 To avoid confusion, the following nomenclature has been followed: Kashmir = the region in India; *kashmir* = a shawl made there. Kashmir shawl = any shawl purporting to come from Kashmir, even when known to be a European imitation. Cashmere (the French spelling) has been avoided, except in quoted passages. Not the least drawback of the term is that it lends colour to the notion that the shawls were more French than Indian – a view hardly credited outside France.
40 *The Compact Edition of the Oxford English Dictionary*, Vol. 2, p. 2774.
41 J. Irwin, *Shawls: a Study in Indo-European Influences*, HMSO 1955, p. 19.
42 P. Clabburn, *Shawls in Imitation of the Indian*, Shire Album 77, Shire Publications 1981, p. 3.
43 *Ibid.*, p. 7.
44 *The Compact Edition of the Oxford English Dictionary*, Vol. 2, p. 2774.
45 J.W. von Goethe, *Travels in Italy . . .*, 1885, p. 199.
46 C. Nicoullaud, ed., *Memoirs of the comtesse de Boigne (1781–84)*, 1907, pp. 84-5.
47 London, Arts Council of Great Britain, *Lady Hamilton in relation to the art of her time*, 1972, p.45.
48 A. Racinet, *Le Costume Historique*, 6 Vols., 1888, Vol. 6, unpaginated.
49 Jouy-en-Josas, Musée Oberkampf, *Impressions Cachemire au XIXe. siècle*, 1984, p. 3.
50 Irwin, *Shawls*, p. 32.
51 *Journal de la Mode et du Goût*, No. 11, 5 June 1790, pp. 1-3.
52 Vigée-Lebrun, *op. cit.*, Vol. 1, p. 27.
53 *Journal des Dames et des Modes*, No. LX, 25 November 1797, p. 7.
54 Ibid., No. XI, 18 November 1798, p. 180.
55 A. Latour, *Kings of Fashion*, Weidenfeld & Nicolson 1958, p. 38.
56 Racinet, *op. cit.*, Vol. 6, unpaginated.

THE SHAWL AS MANUFACTURED PRODUCT
57 Irwin, *The Kashmir Shawl*, p. 21.
58 New Haven, Connecticut, Yale University Art Gallery, *The Kashmir Shawl*, 1975, p. 19.
59 P. Clabburn, *op. cit.*, p. 5.
60 Norfolk Museums Service, *Norwich Shawls*, (exhibition checklist), n.d., p. 1.
61 Yale University Art Gallery, *op. cit.*, pp. 20, 22.
62 M. Blair, *The Paisley Shawl and the men who produced it*, Alexander Gardner 1904, pp. 29-30.
63 Irwin, *The Kashmir Shawl*, p. 19.
64 Clabburn, *op. cit.*, p. 7.
65 *Ibid.*
66 E. Rossbach, *The Art of Paisley*, Van Nostrand Reinhold Co., p. 22.
67 Clabburn, *op. cit.*, pp. 8-9.
68 *Ibid.*, p. 7.
69 *Lady's Monthly Museum* , Vol. 2, January 1799, fig. 2, p. 60.
70 Irwin, *The Kashmir Shawl*, p. 22.
71 F. Irwin, 'The Printed Shawl in Scotland, *c.* 1785–1870', *Costume*, No. 15, 1981, p. 26.
72 *Ibid.*, pp. 26-7.
73 *Ibid.*, p. 26.

CHAPTER 3

THE FRENCH EMPHASIS ON DESIGN

1 Paris, Musée de La Mode et du Costume, *La Mode du Châle Cachemire en France*, 1982, p. 7.
2 Claire de Rémusat, *Mémoirs de Mme de Rémusat 1802–1808*, 3 Vols., Calmann-Lévy n.d., Vol. II, pp. 108–9.

3   Irwin, *Shawls.*, p. 15.
4   K. Clark, *The Romantic Rebellion: romantic versus classic art*, Futura Publications 1976, pp. 133–4.
5   Irwin, *Shawls*, p. 1.
6   *Journal des Dames et des Modes*, No. 53, 15 June 1806, Plate 730; No. 59, 15 July 1806, Plate 737.
7   *Ibid.*, No. 8, 2 November 1803, p. 64.
8   *Ibid.*, No. 7, 5 February 1810, p. 56.
9   Irwin, *Shawls*, pp. 33–4.
10 *Ibid.*, p. 34; Paris, Musée de La Mode et du Costume, *La Mode du Châle Cachemire*, p. 20.
11 Paris, Musée de La Mode et du Costume, *La Mode du Châle Cachemire*, Illustration Nos. 7–9, Catalogue Nos. 26–30.
12 *Ibid.*, pp. 20–1; Lyon, *Le Châle Cachemire en France au XIXe Siècle*, 1983, p. 22.
13 Irwin, *Shawls*, p. 34.
14 Paris, Musée de La Mode et du Costume, *La Mode du Châle Cachemire.*, p. 52.
15 Irwin, *Shawls*, p. 32; A. Adburgham, *Shops and Shopping, 1800–1914*, George Allen & Unwin 1964, p. 98.
16 Adburgham, *op. cit.*, p. 98.

BRITISH SHAWLS: EDINBURGH
17 D. Whyte, 'Edinburgh Shawls and their makers', *Costume*, No. 10, 1976, p. 16.
18 *Ibid.*, p. 23.
19 D. Whyte, 'Paisley Shawls and others', *Costume*, No. 4, 1970, pp. 33, 35.

NORWICH
20 Irwin, *Shawls*, p. 11.
21 *Ibid.*, pp. 20-1.
22 P. Clabburn, *Norwich Shawls*, Information Sheet, Norfolk Museum Services 1977, p. 1.
23 E. McClellan *A History of American Costume, 1607–1870*, Tudor Publishing Co. 1937, pp. 468-9.

SPITALFIELDS
24 C.W. & P. Cunnington, *Handbook of Costume in the 19th Century*, Faber & Faber 1959, p. 364.
25 West Surrey College of Art and Design, *The Art of the Shawl*, 1977. Catalogue No. 112.

PAISLEY
26 C.R. Rock, *Paisley Shawls*, Paisley Museum and Art Galleries 1966, p. 5; *Why Paisley?*, Paisley Museum and Art Galleries, 1985, p. 14.
27 Rock, *op. cit.*, p. 5.
28 Braun-Ronsdorf, *op. cit.*, p. 73.
29 Gernsheim, *op. cit.*, p. 30.
30 Clabburn, *Norwich Shawls*, p.3.

31 A. Buck, *Victorian Costume and Costume Accessories*, Herbert Jenkins 1961, p. 107.
32 Irwin, *The Kashmir Shawl*, p. 25.
33 Boucher, *op. cit.*, p. 396.
34 London, Barbican Art Gallery, *James Tissot*, 1984, Illustration Nos. 4-5, 13-16, Catalogue Nos. 55, 60-1, 81, 83, 110; Buck, *Victorian Costume*, p. 113.

SCARVES AND BOAS
35 Z. Halls, *Machine-made lace in Notingham*, Nottingham Services Committee 1981, pp. 34-7.
36 Cunnington, *A Dictionary of English Costume*, p. 19.
37 A. Ribeiro, 'Furs in Fashion', *Connoisseur*, Vol. 202, No. 814, December 1979, p. 231; the portrait of Mlle Rivière is illustrated in this article.
38 Cunnington, *A Dictionary of English Costume*, p. 229.

CHAPTER 4

FUR AND FEATHERED BOAS

1   E. Ewing, *Fur in Dress*, B.T. Batsford 1981, p. 113.
2   J. Laver, *Taste and Fashion*, George G. Harrap & Co. 1937, p. 103.
3   *Ibid.*, p. 109.
4   Ewing, *op. cit.*, p. 124.
5   A. Lurie, *The Language of Clothes*, Heinemann 1981, p. 234.
6   Ewing, *op. cit.*, pp. 138-9.
7   J. Dorner, *Fashion*, Octopus Books 1974, p. 125 and New York, Metropolitan Museum of Art, *Yves Saint Laurent*, 1983, pp. 166-7, Catalogue No. 162.

SHAWLS
8   Baines, *op. cit.*, p. 95.
9   *Ibid.*, p. 175
10 P. Clabburn, *Norwich Shawls*, p. 3.
11 Paris, Musée de La Mode et du Costume, *'L'Imprimé' dans La Mode du XVIIIe siècle à nos jours*, 1984, p. 72, Catalogue No. 214.

SCARVES
12 P. White, *Poiret*, Studio Vista 1974, p. 83.
13 London, Victoria & Albert Museum, *Four Hundred Years of Fashion*, 1984, p. 82.
14 White, *op. cit.*, p. 86.
15 *Ibid.*, p. 31.
16 *Ibid.*
17 London, Arts Council of Great Britain, *Raoul Dufy 1877–1953*, 1983, pp. 74-86.
18 *Ibid.*, pp. 88, 179, Catalogue No. 391.
19 Lurie, *op. cit.*, p. 181.

Glossary

Materials, manufacturing and decorative techniques not already elucidated in the text

Brocade   a woven textile with a pattern of raised figures which are made by the threads of a different yarn or colour.

Chantilly lace   a bobbin lace made in north-eastern France in the second half of the eighteenth century. It was imitated from about the mid-nineteenth century on the Pusher and Leavers machines.

Chenille   the French name for the hairy caterpillar aptly describes the appearance of this silk or wool yarn with its bristling pile, achieved by weaving the threads standing out at right angles from a core. The technique was invented by a tailor called Scheling during the reign of Louis XV.

China crêpe   thicker than ordinary *crêpe*, it was made from raw silk that was gummed and twisted.

Chiné   a warp-printed silk of which the design appeared to have 'run'. In eighteenth-century England it was called 'clouded lustrings'.

Crêpe   a semi-transparent material with a crinkled surface.

Crêpe de Chine   a very soft China silk *crêpe*, plain or figured, woven from a silk warp and worsted weft.

Drawloom   a handloom with an overhead 'harness' to provide closer control of the warp-threads, allowing the weaving of curvilinear designs, such as floral and cone motifs. A drawboy pulled the harness ropes as instructed by the weaver.

Écru   literally unbleached, but from about 1820 hand-made lace was tinted (sometimes with coffee or tea!) as fashion dictated, to distinguish it from the dazzling white products of machines.

Furbelows   flounces on a dress which are made of the same material.

Gauze   a very thin, transparent material of silk, linen or various types of cotton.

Jacquard loom   named after the Lyonnais inventor, who first exhibited his loom at the Paris Exhibition in 1801, although not introduced commercially in France until about 1810, while at Paisley in common use only from about 1840. Punched cards replaced the drawboy, to make the loom much more mechanized than its predecessor, the drawloom.

Leno   a cotton or silk gauze where two threads of warp which pass between the same splits of the reed are crossed over each other, and twined like a cord at every thread.

Mousseline de soie   a gauze-like silk muslin with an open mesh.

Mull   a very soft, semi-transparent cotton or silk in a plain weave.

Net   a material of fine mesh.

Picot   a small loop of twisted thread used as a decorative edging to lace.

Plaid   long rectangular shawl with a length of ten or twelve feet; a three-quarter plaid is eight feet four inches long.

Plissé   a material chemically treated or resist-printed to produce a crinkled effect.

Robings   trimmings around the neck, bodice and skirts of a dress.

Tambour   a chain-stitch embroidery worked on a circular frame. A hooked needle loops threads of cotton or floss through a material such as net, silk or muslin from the wrong side of the material.

Tulle   a gossamer silk net. It was named after the French city of Tulle where the material was first made. In Britain, the earliest machine-made tulle was produced in Nottingham in 1768.

Twill-tapestry technique   a method of Indian weaving which resembles European tapestry weaving. The pattern is put in with a separate shuttle for each colour, which only goes as far as the pattern requires and then turns back. The only difference is that the ground is a twill instead of a plain weave.

Whitework   a type of embroidery in which white thread is worked on white material. It includes different types of openwork, using cutwork or drawn threads.

Bibliography

REFERENCE

Boucher, F., *20,000 Years of Fashion*, Harry N. Abrams 1966.

Buck, A., *Victorian Costume and Costume Accessories*, Herbert Jenkins 1961.

Cunnington, C.W. & P., *A Dictionary of English Costume*, Adam & Charles Black 1972.
Handbook of English Costume in the 17th Century, Faber & Faber, 3rd ed. 1972.
Handbook of English Costume in the 18th Century, revised ed. 1972.
Handbook of English Costume in the 19th Century, Faber & Faber 1959.

Earnshaw, P., *A Dictionary of Lace*, Shire Publications 1982.

Ribeiro, A., *A Visual History of Costume: The Eighteenth Century*, B.T. Batsford 1983.

GENERAL

Baines, B., *Fashion Revivals*, B.T. Batsford 1981.

Blum. S., ed., *Victorian Fashions & Costumes from Harper's Bazar: 1867-1898*, Dover Publications 1974.

Ewing, E., *Fur in Dress*, B.T. Batsford 1981.

Laver, J., *Taste and Fashion from the French Revolution until today*, George G. Harrap 1937.

Lurie, A., *The Language of Clothes*, Heinemann 1981.

Ribeiro, A., 'Furs in Fashion: the eighteenth and early nineteenth centuries', *Connoisseur*, Vol. 202, No. 814, Dec. 1979.
' "Turquerie": Turkish Dress and English Fashion in the Eighteenth Century', *Connoisseur*, Vol. 201, No. 807, May 1979.

Swain, M.H., 'Nightgown into Dressing Gown: a study of men's nightgowns, 18th century', *Costume*, No. 6, 1972.

Weiss, F., 'Bejewelled Fur Tippets – and the Palatine Fashion', *Costume*, No. 4, 1970.

SPECIFICALLY ON SHAWLS

Blair, M., *The Paisley Shawl and the men who produced it*, Alexander Gardner 1904.

Clabburn, P., *Shawls in Imitation of the Indian*, Shire Publications 1981.

Cross, W., 'Descriptive sketch of the changes in the Style of Paisley Shawls', *The Paisley and Renfrewshire Gazette*, 1892.

Hunter, J., 'The Paisley Textile Industry', *Costume*, No. 10, 1976.

Irwin, F., 'The Printed Shawl in Scotland, *c.* 1785–1870', *Costume*, No. 15, 1981.

Irwin, J., *The Kashmir Shawl*, HMSO 1973.
Shawls: a Study in Indo-European Influences, HMSO 1955.

Leavitt, T.W., 'Fashion Commerce and Technology in the Nineteenth Century: the Shawl Trade, *Textile History*, Vol. 3, Dec. 1972.

Rossbach, E., *The Art of Paisley*, Van Nostrand Reinhold 1980.

Whyte, D., 'Edinburgh Shawls and their makers', *Costume*, No. 10, 1976.
'Paisley shawls and others', *Costume*, No. 4, 1970.

MUSEUM PUBLICATIONS AND EXHIBITION CATALOGUES

London, Victoria & Albert Museum, *Four Hundred Years of Fashion*, 1984.
Hollar to Heideloff, Costume Society 1979.

Los Angeles County Museum of Art, *An Elegant Art*, 1983.

Lyon, Musée Historique des Tissus, *Le Châle Cachemire en France au XIXe siècle,* 1983.

New Haven, Connecticut, Yale University Art Gallery, *The Kashmir Shawl*, 1975.

Paisley Museum and Art Galleries, *Paisley Shawls: a Chapter in the Industrial Revolution* (text by C.R. Rock), 1966.
Why Paisley?, 1985.

Paris, Musée de La Mode et du Costume, *"L' Imprimé" dans La Mode du XVIIIe siècle à nos jours*, 1984.
Indispensables Accessoires, XVIe-XXe siècle, 1984.
La Mode du Châle Cachemire en France, 1982.

West Surrey College of Art and Design, *The Art of the Shawl: an Exhibition of Printed and Woven Shawls from 1780 to the present day*, 1977.

Museums to Visit

Index